P9-DUI-069

# After the Wall

*Confessions from an*
*East German Childhood and*
*the Life that Came Next*

## Jana Hensel

translated by Jefferson Chase

**PUBLICAFFAIRS**
New York

Copyright © 2004 by Jana Hensel

Originally published under the title *Zonenkinder*
Copyright © 2002 by Rowohlt Verlag GmbH,
Reinbek bei Hamburg.

Published in the United States by PublicAffairs™,
a member of the Perseus Books Group.
All rights reserved.
Printed in the United States of America.

No part of this book may be reproduced in any manner whatsoever without
written permission except in the case of
brief quotations embodied in critical articles and reviews. For information,
address PublicAffairs, 250 West 57th Street, Suite 1321, New York, NY 10107.
PublicAffairs books are available at special discounts for bulk purchases in
the U.S. by corporations, institutions, and other organizations. For more
information, please contact the Special Markets Department at the Perseus
Books Group, 2300 Chestnut Street, Suite 200, Philadelphia, PA 19103, or
call (800) 255-1514, or e-mail special.markets@perseusbooks.com.

Book design by Jane Raese

Library of Congress Cataloging-in-Publication Data
Hensel, Jana.
[Zonenkinder. English]
After the Wall : confessions from an East German childhood and the life that
came next / Jana Hensel ; translated by Jefferson Chase.
p. cm.
HC: ISBN 1-58648-266-1
PB: ISBN 978-1-58648-559-7

1. Hensel, Jana. 2. Teenage girls—Germany (East)—Biography. 3. Teenage
girls—Germany (East). 4. Youth—Germany (East). 5. Germany—Politics and
government—1990- I. Title.
HQ799.G3H45613 2004
943.087'092—dc22
2004053549

10 9

# Contents

# Contents

# Timeline of the GDR and of Jana Hensel's Life

*May 1945*   WWII ends. The Soviet Army captures Berlin and accepts Germany's surrender. The city is divided into four separate zones controlled by Britain, France, the United States, and the Soviet Union.

*June 1948–May 1949*   As tensions rise between the new superpowers, the Soviet forces blockade West Berlin, trapping its inhabitants with little food or fuel. West Berlin is an island inside Communist-controlled East Germany, and the Allies keep the city alive with a continuous airlift of supplies.

*May 23, 1949*   The Federal Republic of Germany—West Germany—is founded.

*October 7, 1949*   The German Democratic Republic (GDR)—East Germany—is founded.

*1952*   East Germany closes its borders with West

## Timeline

Germany. Only the border between East and West Berlin remains.

*June 1953*   Mass uprising of East Berlin building workers against the Communist government. The revolt is crushed with the help of the Soviet Army. At least forty people are killed.

*August 11, 1961*   Berliners hear rumors of the Soviet Union closing the border. More than 4,000 East Germans flee to West Berlin.

*August 12–13, 1961*   East German troops seal Berlin's borders and begin building the Wall on the night of August 12. The Wall begins as a barbed wire barrier and gradually grows into an elaborate series of walls and fences, fortified with automatically triggered weapons and patrolled by heavily armed guards with dogs, all designed to stop East Germans from leaving. In the years that follow, more than 200 people are killed trying to cross the Wall.

*August 26, 1961*   All crossing points are closed to West Berlin citizens.

*June 26, 1963*  President Kennedy visits the Wall. He pronounces himself a "Berliner" and pledges to defend the residents of West Berlin.

*May 1973*  East Germany and West Germany establish formal diplomatic ties.

*1976*  Jana Hensel is born in the GDR.

*1983–1990*  Jana Hensel attends grade school in Leipzig

*June 12, 1987*  President Reagan visits Berlin and urges Soviet leader Mikhail Gorbachev to tear down the Wall.

*May–September 1989*  Hungary opens its borders with Austria, allowing East Germans to begin leaving the Eastern Bloc. East Germans begin taking refuge in West German embassies in Poland, Czechoslovakia, and Hungary.

*September 10, 1989*  Hungarian government stops enforcing East German visa restrictions, opening its borders. In the first three days, 15,000 East

## Timeline

German refugees pass through en route to West Germany, where they receive asylum.

*September–October 1989*   In the face of weekly pro-democracy demonstrations that begin in the city of Leipzig, Communist leader Erich Honecker is forced to resign as head of state and is replaced by professed reformist Egon Krenz.

*November 4, 1989*   An anti-Communist protest in East Berlin draws more than one million people demanding democracy. Three days later, the East German government resigns.

*November 9, 1989*   The Berlin Wall is opened, and travel restrictions are lifted. Mass celebrations follow.

*December 1989*   Chancellor Helmut Kohl begins Round Table talks with new East German leader, Hans Modrow.

*February 1990*   The Soviet Union, Britain, France, and the United States approve reunification.

*March 18, 1990*   In free elections, East Germans

overwhelmingly approve reunification and Western-style political and economic systems. A formal treaty is signed in May.

*October 3, 1990*   Germany is formally reunited.

*1991–1995*   Jana Hensel attends high school in Leipzig as part of the first East German class to use a Western syllabus.

*1998–1999*   Jana spends a year in Marseilles.

*1999*   Jana moves to Berlin.

*2002*   Jana moves to Paris for one year, then back to Berlin. She begins to write *After the Wall*.

*2002*   *After the Wall* is published in Germany as *Zonenkinder*. Book debuts on the bestseller list and stays there from September 2002 until March 2004, including ten months in the top ten. *Zonenkinder* is reprinted fourteen times. More than 180,000 copies are sold in Germany.

*2004*   Paperback edition of *Zonenkinder* is published in Germany and becomes an immediate bestseller. Companion volume of essays on "the book that changed Germany" is published under the title *Zonenkinder und Wir* (*"Zonenkinder and Us"*).

# 1. That Warm Fuzzy Feeling of Togetherness:
## On Growing Up in the GDR

My childhood ended one evening when I was thirteen years and three months old. It was already dark when Mom and I left the house. Dark and cold. We could see our breath in front of our faces. I had been told to put on tights, boots, and two sweaters underneath my blue thermal anorak, but no one told me where we were going. We crossed over the railroad tracks to get to the tram stop to downtown Leipzig. We didn't see a single soul. At least, I don't think we did. Now, when I look back, I can't honestly remember whether the streets were really deserted or whether I just imagine them that way. And I can't say for sure that I appreciated the beauty of the rain, just barely visible in the yellow-gray glow of the streetlights.

Back then, you had to open tram doors by hand, and they didn't shut tight. An ice-cold draft would blow in through the cracks, while you burned your butt on the overheated leather seats. That night, the passengers in the streetcar were all bundled up in heavy outdoor clothing. A few women wore those fashionable earmuffs that had just recently appeared in the shops. Others wore legwarmers that they had knitted by hand. I thought it was weird that no one was carrying a handbag.

After several stops, the driver opened the doors of the first car and told us the tram was being terminated. We'd have to walk the rest of the way. We all got out and headed off, without a word, in the same direction—as if there were only one possible destination that evening.

As we arrived in the center of town, I saw crowds of people forcing their way toward St. Nicolas Church and Karl Marx Square. There were masses of people lined up to march along the ring road. Some carried banners and signs. I can't be sure any more what I saw with my own eyes and what I now remember from the endless newscasts that followed. But I'm certain—probably because I never discussed them with anyone—that a few of my recollections are personal. I remember walking beside a university student and wanting to hold his hand. And I remember the armed men in uniform standing on the side of the road watching us; I wanted to ask them why they didn't come join us. After all, there were a lot more of us than there were of them.

Instead I just kept walking, like a good girl, between my mother and the student. For the first time in my life, I realized that something big was happening—something I didn't understand. Even the grown-ups seemed confused. What would all this lead to? If the student had told me that this was just the beginning, that with each successive Monday more and more people would take to the streets, that the walls would fall and the German Democratic Republic—Communist East Germany—would soon disappear without a trace, taking everything we had known with it, I would have given him a funny look and thought: Fat chance. The GDR couldn't disappear. Not in a million years.

There was no way for me to know that fall of 1989 that I was living the last days of my childhood. Now, when I look back on those years before the Wall fell and the whole world changed around us, it seems like a far-away, fairy-tale time. It's a remote past with different hairstyles, different smells, and a different pace of life. It's not easy for people my age—the last generation of GDR kids—to remember the old days, because back then we wanted nothing more than for them to hurry up and end—as though there would be no pain whatsoever involved in losing everything we knew. At some point the tram doors shut properly, and the old days were suddenly gone.

Now, a decade and a half later, the first half of our lives seems very remote. Even when we try, we can't remember much. Nothing remains of our childhood country—which is of course exactly what everyone wanted—and now that we're grown up and it's almost too late, I suddenly miss all the lost memories. I've grown afraid that, by always looking forward and never glancing back, we no longer have any idea where we stand. I'd like to retrace where we come from, to rediscover lost memories and forgotten experiences. I only worry whether I'll be able to find my way back.


Shortly after the Wall fell in November 1989, the pictures of Lenin and former GDR Head of State and Party Erich Honecker disappeared from our classrooms. It was all we could talk about for a while. Day in and day out, these two men had been as much a part of our visual lives as the test pattern that appeared on television at the end of the broadcast day, but we only really noticed them after they were gone.

A bit later, the old system of buying milk collectively—paying a month in advance and having it delivered to your home—was discontinued. Presumably, the change was made to avoid scaring off new customers in a free market economy, but I don't remember exactly when it happened. What I do remember was that moment of rebellion years before—it must have been in the second or third grade—when, behind the teacher's back, I tore open the slippery and always somewhat smelly plastic milk package with my teeth and drank straight from the hole. That was cool. The others were still drinking their milk through straws like kindergartners.

At some other point in late '89 or early '90—here, too, I can't remember exactly when—we stopped going to all those state-run extracurricular events. Saturdays had previously been reserved for community activities, but now most of us preferred to drive across the border to West Germany with our parents to pick up our *Begrüssungsgeld*—the 100 deutschmarks in "welcome money" handed out by the West German government to East German visitors. Our teachers soon decided to do the same. Saturday activities were never officially discontinued; they simply disappeared on their own. The same thing happened to Tuesday afternoons. No one was interested in dance fitness groups, the Young Historians Society, the chess club, or art classes anymore. And Wednesdays changed, too. As a pre-teen in the GDR, I used to put on my red scarf and pointy cap every Wednesday afternoon at 4 P.M., and head off to meetings of the *Junge Pioniere* (Young Pioneers), our version of the Scouts, but with a heavy Socialist slant. Likewise, the older kids used to attend gatherings of the *Freie Deutsche Jugend,* or Free German Youth.

One by one, we stopped all the activities through which our Socialist pedagogues had hoped to mold our personalities and to prepare us for future careers as engineers, cos-

A Young Pioneer in uniform.
The three red stripes on her sleeve
signify high office.

monauts, teachers, or transportation workers. Contact lapsed between us and the industrial managers
who had served as our state-sponsored godfathers
and who were responsible for initiating us into the
mysteries of Socialist production. The milk-money
collector disappeared, as did the group committee
director, his deputy, and the leader of the Young
Pioneers.

Seemingly overnight, the endless appointments
that had filled our childhood were cancelled. We
used to arrive at school to find that a short excur-
sion, a fire alarm, or a flag saluting exercise had
been scheduled before first period. No more. The
compulsory medical examinations were discontinued, and no one accompanied us—for reasons of
"class solidarity," as our teachers had always said—
down to the school basement, where the dentist had
set up a makeshift office. That was all right with
me. I was just as happy not to have to wait on the
long, hard sports benches and listen to the dentist
drilling in the next room, or to sprint back up the
stairs holding my nose so as not to gag on the smell
of antiseptics.

Gone, too, were the Spartacus Track and Field
Competitions. No one came to tell us where to set
up the heavy black loudspeakers, which would kick

off the big event by blaring the Olympic anthem. It was the end of a childhood ritual. Track meets were huge in the GDR. They always started around 7 A.M., before the sun had even come up. We would stand around the freezing sports fields, anxiously awaiting our chance to qualify for the district championships in the triple jump or the sixty-meter dash. I would press the thermos of hot tea clipped to my belt against my belly and imagine the voice of Heinz Florian Oertel, East Germany's leading sports announcer, relating my triumphs. Others would slap their biceps, as they had seen our national cyclists do on television during the last Goodwill Games with the West.

Competitive sports were out. No one went to after-school practice any more. We'd always been irritated that sports had clashed with the ever-exciting *Little House on the Prairie* or the 1950s Western series *Fury*. (Everyone in the GDR watched Western TV shows, which could be picked up by fiddling with the TV antennas. We just had to do it secretively, and we were careful never to mention our favorite shows in front of our teachers.) Kids used to get back home at 6 P.M., exhausted and sore, chug a bottle of milk in front of the refrigerator, and then quickly do homework. Now we rushed home as soon as school was over and parked ourselves in front of the TV. Our mothers initially welcomed this development. At long last, there'd be time to watch *Medicine by Numbers, Monika the Jockey, Suburban Hospital* and other GDR shows as a family. The only problem was that, by the time we stopped going to after-school sports in 1990, those shows had all been cancelled.

The ABC magazines for young readers gradually disappeared from our school, taking with them *Manne Murmelauge,* the friendly little freckle-faced mascot with the scarf and cap from page three, who gave us tips on how to better organize our charity fund-raising brigades, or how to improve the quality of our special edition of the school newspaper celebrating the signing of the Warsaw Pact. No longer did Manne explain the meaning of the three points of the Young Pioneer neck scarf or urge us to recycle old newspapers and hold bake sales in our school lobby to raise funds for Nelson Mandela and the Sandinistas. Bake sales, according to Manne in

The Young Pioneer mascot, Manne Murmelauge.

the old days, were best staged in front of the principal's office and the door leading to the school playground, where the flags of the GDR, the Young Pioneers, the Free German Youth, and the Soviet Union would be clearly visible. If we won the competition between schools for the most money raised, Manne had always promised, we'd win a pennant, and Mandela would get to leave jail.

Frankly, I could see the advantage in not having Manne around any more telling us what to do. I'd always been an enthusiastic collector of old newspapers: the SERO recycling company had paid a couple of cents per kilo, and it had been one of the few ways to earn a bit of extra pocket money. But in a free market economy, you had to collect two to three times as much paper before they'd buy it, and competition for territory was fierce. If we had rung a doorbell and announced "Hello, we're from the Young Pioneers, and we're collecting old bottles and newspapers" on a street that belonged to the seventh-grade kids, there would have been trouble. When we went around collecting old paper, we'd post the toughest-looking kid in front of the house to guard our push-cart. If the seventh graders caught us on their turf, then that kid was left to defend our recyclables, while the rest of us scattered.

# That Warm Fuzzy Feeling of Togetherness

Walks through the woods were more dangerous after 1989. I no longer had Korbine Früchtchen, the mascot of the FRÖSI "Let's Be Joyful and Sing" Society, at my side to tell me which berries were okay to eat and which weren't. She used to explain that the forestry industry depended on me to collect chestnuts and acorns, and to plant medicinal herbs in the school garden to increase its annual production. But our interests had moved on anyway: We now collected the free toy surprises that came with McDonald's Happy Meals. We no longer spent our Sunday afternoons making acorn figures or decorating our bicycle spokes with beer coasters. We now sat inside hunched over a game of Monopoly or absorbed in a Mickey Mouse comic book.


Today, when I look at old GDR photos of myself, I see a sulky kid with an old leather military pouch slung haphazardly over her shoulders and a white nurse's bonnet with a Red Cross insignia on her head, her hands tightly gripping the handlebars of a green push-bike. In those pictures, I'm always staring directly into the camera. If I didn't know better, I'd say I looked a bit like an operative in some child police commando. That was one of the by-products of an ideological education—children learned that they were supposed to be useful and do their duty toward the state. As kids, we were always pretending to be soldiers, nurses, cops, doctors—any responsible job where you got to wear a uniform.

These pictures were taken more than fifteen years ago. In the meantime, everything has changed. The Wall came down, the GDR was swallowed up by the West, and my childhood disappeared. Sometimes I feel as if my past has been locked away in a museum with no name and no address, and no one seems very interested in going inside to have a look to see what's there. Occasionally I walk around its dingy rooms. When I do, I stumble across old friends like Manne Murmelauge. I'm happy to see him, but I can tell that he resents me for turning my back on him without so much as a goodbye. Indeed, the harder I press my nose to his glass case, the more he seems to withdraw from view.

As soon as the Wall fell, the language changed. The consumer depot was suddenly called a "supermarket," nickies became "T-shirts," and apprentices turned into "trainees." Counters were called "terminals," the Polylux machine became an "overhead projector," and date books had morphed into "Filofaxes." One morning, after the local polyclinic had gotten a fresh coat of paint, the sign over the door suddenly read "Doctors' Offices." And *mondos* were now known as "condoms"—but that didn't concern us at our age. Not yet.

I no longer went to the Pioneer House but to the rec center, where the Pioneer Leaders were now called "supervisors." Before, our activities were organized into so-called working groups; now everybody just joined "clubs."

In stores you could buy everything that was advertised on TV. Everywhere on the streets, con men were trying to get suckers to bet money on shell games. Ex-classmates who'd fled the GDR before the fall of the Wall—who'd "absconded," as people used to say—now reappeared in our schoolyards, as if they'd never been away. Their accents were different, though, and they looked if they'd just stepped straight out of *Medi&Zini* or one of those other West German kids' TV shows.

We were no longer allowed to call people "Fidschis"; we were told to say "foreigners" or "asylum seekers"; that sounded funny, because many of those people had been born in East Germany and had never been out of the country. We didn't have a special nickname for people from Cuba or Mozambique either, before or after the Wall. And now we didn't need one; after the Wall, they all suddenly disappeared. The same was true for the convicts who used to man the SERO recycling centers, sorting the bottles by color and making sure that none of us climbed through a hole in the fence and broke into the metal container where the Western newspapers were kept, waiting to be re-used for the good of the Socialist community. One day, they too were gone.

I quickly purged my vocabulary of words like "Assis" or "antisocials," which was how we described criminals or people who refused to work. In school, we used to tutor their children, seeing to it that they learned to read and write and that no one picked on them too much. If they played hooky, it was our responsibility to go to their homes and find them. But after the Wall, both the "antisocials" and their kids also disappeared.

With the Olsen family it was different. The Olsens were a band of rather simpleminded Danes, who were the stars of our Sunday morning children's movie matinees. Generations of Socialist kids had laughed at the Olsens' numbskull adventures, mistakenly believing that the presence of Danish films on our screens meant that the world outside the Warsaw Pact hadn't completely forgotten we existed. After the Wall, you could still sometimes catch an old Olsens' film on TV, but it broke my heart to learn that we were the only ones who had ever tuned in. No one in West Germany had even heard of Egon, Benny, and Kjeld. By contrast everyone knew Karel Gott, the "Golden Voice of Prague," whose schmaltzy easy-listening records were a fixture of the state-run East German label Amiga. That was devastating. We always thought Gott had learned German especially for us.

Today, I can't help feeling a bit jealous when my West German friends go on about how much they love going home for visits with their folks. Even though they would never dream of moving back to Heidelberg or Krefeld, it's nice to have everything just as they remember it. That always makes me imagine walking the streets of my childhood, retracing my route to school and rediscovering past sights and smells. I picture myself surreptitiously lying down between periods on the pile of dusty mattresses in the far corner of our school gym and pressing my nose against the heavy medicine ball. I look over at the long wooden benches, run my hand over their surfaces, and remember being afraid of getting splinters when we slid across them on our bellies, churning our arms as if swimming.

To tell the truth, though, I preferred *Völkerball*, a Socialist variation of dodge-ball. There would always be one star who rose to glory when most of his teammates were "out" and the uncoordinated or fat kids who couldn't care less which team won had already headed for the changing rooms. That was too bad for them. They never got to witness how a single star player can completely turn around a game of *Völkerball*. Those of us who stuck around until the end always admired the star. Later, during classes, I would turn round and watch him out of the corner of my eye, basking in his reflected glow.

Yesterday's dodge-ball heroes are gone, and since our childhood has been locked up in that nameless museum, there are no words left to describe them adequately. And because the museum also has no address, I don't even know where to go to find them.

We'll never be part of a youth movement, I thought. It was 1998 and I was spending a year abroad as a university student. I was crowded together with friends from Italy, Spain, France, Germany, and Austria in a tiny dorm room in Marseilles. The Italians had cooked dinner. There were no stools, and people knelt, sat on the bed, squatted on the floor, or simply leaned on the doorframe. After several bottles of wine and enough cigarettes to overflow every ashtray, the mood turned euphoric. Everyone began to jabber at once. The names of childhood heroes ricocheted like balls off the walls. My friends invoked their favorite Smurfs and discussed the genealogical complexities of Smurf Village. Favorite movies were cited, favorites books compared, and heated debates broke out over *The Lord of the Rings* and *Pippi Longstocking*, Donald Duck and Lucky Luke, Asterix and Obelix.

All I had to contribute were Alfons Zitterbacke, well-behaved Ottokar, the Wizard of Sapphire City, and a host of other obscure characters from East German children's books and TV programs. Nobody knew them in the West, of course, but I, too, wanted to share something of my childhood heroes. I tried to explain. The others looked at me with vague interest, but the euphoria was gone. Suddenly I felt sick and tired of being different than everyone else. I just wanted to tell childhood stories—like the Italians, French, and Austrians did—

without having to explain, without having to translate my memories into words that had not been part of my experience and that scattered my recollections even more so with each attempt at clarification. I didn't want to spoil the party and their warm, fuzzy feeling of togetherness, so I just kept my mouth shut. Instead I asked myself: What was I ever going to make of my childhood? Like an old summer dress, it had gone out of fashion. It wasn't even good enough for a bit of party chit-chat. I took a sip of wine and decided it was time to go. Time for a trip. A trip back to where I came from.

## 2. Gateway to Nowhere:

### On Searching for Home

"Ladies and gentlemen, in a few minutes we'll be
approaching Leipzig Central Train Station. Change
here for connections to . . ." The conductor on the
Intercity Express Train between Hamburg and Munich had trouble pronouncing the names of villages
in Saxony. I couldn't blame him. It was difficult for
non-natives to get their tongues around Slavic
sounding names like Eutritzsch, Delitzsch, Meusel-
witz, and Schkeuditz. That made me feel good. It
made me feel at home.

I stood up with some of the other passengers,
gathered my things, and got ready to leave the
train. Maybe it was just my imagination, but I
couldn't help thinking that those who were traveling on to Nuremberg or Munich took a longer,
harder look at those of us who were getting out in
Leipzig than the people who alighted at the West
German stations.

## After the Wall

It was 1999. Until the late 1990s, the Intercity Express Trains that passed through Leipzig were mostly empty. You never had to reserve a seat. But ever since the Hamburg-Munich train was re-routed through East Germany, the cars had been full to capacity. I was proud that people on their way to Oktoberfest or the North Sea, all the skiers and the beachgoers, now had to travel through our country. Beyond the city of Jena, the southbound train chugs through the picturesque Saal Valley and past Dornburg Castle. A real estate developer from Bavaria once dubbed this stretch of land the Tuscany of the GDR. I was sure my fellow passengers would appreciate its beauty.

But, as I eavesdropped on a conversation between some Bavarian retirees, all I heard was shock and dismay at the high-rise housing blocks in the city suburbs, and the derelict factories in former industrial centers like Wolfen or Bitterfeld. They couldn't get over their ingrained contempt for the Communist system. "It's hard to imagine," they were saying, "how people could have survived here. Thank God, the dark days are over." When I heard that, I wanted to get up, go over to their seats, and set them straight—things had not been quite *that* bad.

I'm sure if they'd stopped in Leipzig, they would

at least have liked the train station. Leipzig *Haupt-bahnhof* is not only a reassuring example of nascent East German prosperity; it's also a hugely popular new temple of consumerism. Following Cologne and Hanover's example, Leipzig built a massive, glitzy convention complex in 1996 and renamed itself "Convention City." The train station followed suit. In the passenger lounge they play cheesy music by West German pop stars from the 1980s, and all the stores are open until 10 P.M., seven days a week. If you light up a cigarette, three security guards will run up and tell you to put it out. In Leipzig *Haupt-bahnhof* everything has turned out the way it was intended. Even the homeless shelter has been closed so that the sight of vagrants won't spoil the glossy image of the new, revitalized East.

When it first opened after the renovations, people's love for their new train station knew no bounds. Folks came in droves from all over the state of Saxony just to have a look. Rail officials had hastily hung up some posters with pictures of other major European cities like Milan and Amsterdam. "You see," the posters seemed to say, "you can travel from here to every corner of the globe." The visitors seemed convinced. Back then, I thought it was a bit sad for us locals, after all the effort we'd put in and after three construction workers had lost their lives constructing the colossus, that the German Chancellor couldn't attend the re-opening ceremony. It was foggy that day, and his helicopter was unable to land, so he just headed back up into the clouds.

But things had changed in the last three years. Leipzig *Hauptbahnhof*, I discovered, was no longer *our* train station. We hadn't set off from there to discover the wide world, any more than people had done from the ritzy new train stations in Dresden or East Berlin. Instead unemployed people offered, through gritted teeth, to carry my bags, and railway employees struggled to maintain the proper tone of absolute servility. For us, these redecorated stations have become foreign territory. Unlike the buildings that previously stood on their sites, they neither opened up a gateway to the world nor welcomed us back home.

Nor was Leipzig itself the city I remembered. No sooner had I shown my first Western visitors the renovated Maedler Arcades, or recounted the story of real-estate developer Jürgen Schneider and his spectacular bankruptcy and corruption trial, or

A West German journalist posing as a West German journalist
for a West German magazine right after the fall of the Wall.
Authentic stories about East Germany were everywhere.
You just had to arrange them.

taken my guests around to experience East Germany's liveliest bar scene, than I said goodbye to
the city of my childhood. I was proud of the
spruced-up apartment houses and the new shopping malls, stores, and bike paths, but I couldn't

shake the feeling that the experiences my visitors craved were things they had read about in magazines like *Der Spiegel* and *Focus*. They wanted the old stuff. As long as you took them to the Secret Police Museum, and showed them St. Nicholas Church, where all the Monday night demonstrations had taken place in 1989, carefully pointing out where the surveillance cameras had been placed to monitor those demonstrations, they were happy. And, once you told a couple of personal anecdotes (ideally in Saxon dialect), the visitors decided they'd found what they'd been after. And off they'd go to their next stop in another city in the former Communist East.

Sadly for us, our country disappeared when we told these stories. In the mistaken belief that anecdotes were the stuff from which our new lives were made, we convinced ourselves that we liked telling our stories and even began exchanging them amongst ourselves. In the process, we lost touch with our true experiences, and one memory after another slipped away. Places like St. Nicholas Church as the site of the Monday Rallies or the *Stasi* Museum were not part of our childhood. They are symbols of its ending—of the demise of the GDR. Just as you tell a love story differently, depending on whether it has a happy or a tragic ending, in the 1990s we always related the history of the GDR as a tale of failure—a country doomed to extinction, which had experienced only rare moments of rebellion.

After the Wall, we soon forgot what everyday life in the GDR was like, with all its unheroic moments and ordinary days. We repressed our actual experiences and replaced them with a series of strange, larger-than-life anecdotes that didn't really have anything to do with what our lives had been like. The fact that we began exchanging such stories amongst ourselves shows how much we had internalized the West German take on our history. We had forgotten how to tell our own life stories in our own way, instead adopting an alien tone and perspective.

Visitors especially loved walking around the mines and the slagheaps that extended along nearly the entire southern perimeter of the city. They wanted to see for themselves what they called the "environmental devastation." Even as the few remaining miners were still busy at the site digging coal, visitors would admire the cranes and conveyer belts, which now stood rusty and disused. Here were the steel monuments of the bygone Industrial

Age. I always moved off a bit to one side, so as not
to disturb this grandiose image. For me, the mines
were just another familiar sight. I knew a lot of people who still drove to work every morning along
the lone street that led from their homes to the
chemical plant.

My high school was located on the other side of
the slag pit. I was surprised that it hadn't been torn
down. The mine began directly behind the school
gymnasium and, if you hung out in the schoolyard,
after a little while you could feel the dust and the
sand grinding between your teeth. Our bicycles
were always covered with dust—the boys would
curse because it messed up the gears. At night, the
boarding students whose windows looked out on
the mine sometimes would dream of the blue light
that came from the conveyer belts, which you could
see for miles.

I hated strolling about in my own life like a
tourist, admiring the machines and reducing my
own biography to a handful of anecdotes I knew my
Western visitors wanted to hear—or thought that
they wanted to hear. Our childhood wasn't about
environmental devastation or unsafe housing standards. We had grown up in Laundromats, under
chestnut trees, and zipping home from school on

roller skates. We had never lived life in the renovated apartment buildings, the glass-and-steel office complexes, and the monotonous commercial
streets that took over our city during the 1990s.
For us, nothing had ever happened there.

I just couldn't get used to the change. I was always on the look-out for drawings and paintings we
had made as children. I wanted to find out about
the things we had seen back then with our own
eyes. Often, when traveling around East Germany,
I would hold my thumbs and index fingers in front
of my face like a camera frame and scan the streets
and the rows of houses for a snapshot of something
from the GDR. I stared at whatever I had captured
within my frame and tried to think about the old
days; and in the end, I always ended up admitting
my attempt had failed. The feeling of childhood was
never there. As soon as I took my hand down, I'd
find myself in another kind of time capsule. Wherever I looked, I saw the 1990s. It was as though East
Germany had never known any other decade. The
1960s, '70s, and '80s had been renovated away in
the blink of an eye. It was different in West Germany. West Germany was full of hokey architec-
ture—the post offices in Wiesbaden, the breweries
in Cologne, the shoe stores in Erlangen, and the bus

stops in Frankfurt—that proved that past decades had existed and that showed me what they looked like. East Germany was, in comparison, utterly un-differentiated.

When I went home to visit my parents, I took the tram from Leipzig *Hauptbahnhof* to the edge of the city where I grew up and where they still lived. "Next stop: Augustusplatz. Change here for connections to the city center and the suburbs," intoned a computerized voice at an unpleasant volume. No one in the tram car except me, a couple of retirees, and some screaming school kids changed trains. Three video monitors, hung from the ceiling of the cars, broadcast undulating images of the area and announced that the Saxony export was increasing day by day. I wasn't familiar with the phrase "the Saxony export"—which designated the trend of East Germans emigrating to the West—but I wasn't surprised that such an unflattering picture of the city was being shown on its public transportation system. As I'd seen in Leipzig *Hauptbahnhof*, East Germans loved hi-tech gadgetry, and the news, while bad, at least showed that we were leading the way in something.

My tram connection was held up for a while, so I was able to take a close look at Augustusplatz, formerly known as Karl Marx Square. In the old days, this was the center of Leipzig University. The highrise administration building was a city landmark, a fixture of postcards sent from the city before the fall of the Wall. During the 1990s, a persistent rumor circulated—that the people of Leipzig had nicknamed the building, which was designed to look like an opened book, the "Wisdom Tooth." That surprised me. No one I knew had ever used this smug, not particularly clever phrase. The building had been renovated and was now owned by a bank. There was a sign on the roof in black, red, and gold with the Central German Broadcasting Company's logo. It looked like the East German flag without the hammer and calipers, I thought, but the doors of my tram connection were about to close, so I hurried on board.

We passed the student center and local municipal library, leaving the city proper for the southern suburbs. Suddenly, I could have just as well been in East Berlin, Chemnitz, or Gera. The neighborhood looked like any run-of-the-mill East German suburb. It had countless no-name discount stores, bric-a-brac retailers, and cut-rate drugstores. You'd have thought that East Germans spent their entire lives in the kitchen or the bath, only venturing into the rest of their apartments when there was cleaning to be done.

The deserted storefront windows of the Mom-and-Pop shops that couldn't compete were covered with faded advertisements that marked, like gravestones, the dead dreams of small-time entrepreneurs. Someone should collect posters like these, I thought, and make them into an illustrated book about the first decade of reunified Germany. What had happened to all the Maiks and Silvias and Ronnies and Susis who once thought they could get rich by opening their own stationery store, tattoo studio, or snack shop?

Lost in ruminations about the fates of such unknown entrepreneurs, I soon arrived at my parents' house. "Moritzhof," said the computerized voice. "This train terminates here. All passengers please exit. Thank you for using Leipzig public transport." My childhood tram stop had always been called "Watestrasse." I loved the name as a girl precisely because I had no idea what it meant. Now they'd renamed it after a new shopping center.

That shopping center had become the new heart of economic, social, and cultural life in the prefab

suburb where I grew up—and a place for me to
avoid. One of my old classmates worked at the
check-out counter of the supermarket. I never knew
when I was going to run into a former teacher in
line at the butcher's. And the man who made us
scrape our plates in the school cafeteria, and whom
the seventh-grade hooligans used to terrorize, now
just wandered around aimlessly. I didn't want to
come across any of these people. I wanted them to
stay between the pages of the photo albums, where
I'd put them so many years ago.

The street in front of the shopping center was
named for Johannes R. Becher—the guy who wrote
the words to the East German national anthem. It
was never a very nice-looking street, but it had always been a main neighborhood thoroughfare. My
parents' house was at one end, next to an apartment
complex made of prefabricated concrete blocks and
also named after Becher. At the other end of the
street was my grade school.

I paused to consider that I had attended this
school for eight years, and then calculated what
that meant. There were 365 days in a year, for the
first four years I had taken part in vacation activities at school, and on Pioneer days I actually went
to school twice. All told, this meant that I had made

my way up and down Johannes-R.-Becher-Straße more than 5,000 times in my lifetime. Five thousand short walks past the municipal library and the drink shop, saying hello every morning and good-bye every afternoon to my classmates. I knew every slab of concrete in the sidewalk. On the way home from classes, we would play games of either trying to avoid stepping on the cracks or deliberately treading upon them—depending on our moods.

But the street I knew so well was gone. Where I had once walked, there were now benches and huge concrete spheres—some sort of public art project—and kids played street ball in the road. All of the stations of my childhood had disappeared or been drastically made over. Our school cafeteria, a huge concrete block, had been torn down to make room for a parking lot. The landfill behind the apartment complex, where we'd ridden our bikes and con-structed play houses, had been cleared to make way for a fitness center. Home was a place we only knew for a short time.

When in a foreign country, you're automatically drawn to the people who think most like you do, and during my year abroad—this was almost ten years after the Wall—I found I had the most in common with Austrians. They knew what it was like to come from a small nation, and they laughed off being continually mistaken for Germans. By contrast, it took me a long time to accept being regarded as German. Back in the GDR, I had always hoped that people would assume that I was from somewhere in the West. In fact, it wasn't until the first time someone asked me where I was from, which must have been seven years after the Wall, that I suddenly realized how conspicuous East Germans must have been back then when we took our holidays in Poland, Hungary, or Bulgaria. All the other nationalities were easy to peg. You could recognize Polish tourists, even when they weren't packed into their Polish Fiats, by their homemade shoulder bags with their fake Adidas logos and ironed-on Depeche Mode patches. Soviet girls wore brown school uniforms and big pink ribbons in their hair, and they usually had guys with square jaws, Slavic faces, and flat noses at their sides. Czechs favored canvas sneakers with red and blue stripes, stuffed their faces with oblaten cookies, and drove Skodas. Hungarians were good looking, elegant, and snobbish toward the rest of the Communist bloc—the reflected glow of Habsburg monarchy made them think they were something better.

You never saw Bulgarians and Romanians outside their own countries and, as children, we were unsure whether Albanians and Yugoslavians even existed at all, or whether our teachers at school had just made them up. They never came to our country, and we never went to theirs, which we thought was a shame. After all, they were our Communist brothers.

What was it that marked us as East Germans? After all, we considered ourselves the most Western country of Eastern Europe. Was it our four-stroke Trabbi and Wartburg cars or our open-faced, Birkenstock-like sandals that gave us away? I had no idea.

After the Wall, I didn't want to admit that I was German, and I no longer wanted people to think that I came from the West. When I went to France in 1998, I was always reluctant to tell people I was from Germany because they always assumed I meant West Germany. I came from the German Democratic Republic—a separate country with a different history. I tried to explain the difference to my French peers, but I could tell that they really weren't interested in such historical "details." In the

The German Democratic Republic divided by district. The hole in the middle is West Berlin.

end, I just gave up and started referring to myself as German. Ironically it was the French—surely without any intention on their part—who helped me convert to my new nationality. During that year abroad, I was forever qualifying and explaining my identity, and the people on the receiving end of these explanations digested the information—that although I was German, I really came from Leipzig in East Germany, *i.e.,* the former GDR . . . —with what might be described as well-meaning disinterest. In many cases, that reaction was well founded. My next-door neighbor in the dormitory in Marseilles, an Algerian woman, called home every night to find out if any of her family had been killed in the daily massacres back then. There was no reason for her to be interested in differences between East

and West. Germany was a wealthy country.
She probably understood that the majority of East
Germans felt like second-class citizens and that
many of us were out of work—but she'd experienced far worse. That was why I concentrated on
Austrians, especially when I needed an audience
for my lectures on the differences between East
and West.

There was more going on in the East, I pro-
claimed, at least more ideas. People who had to get
used to a new system viewed it more critically.
They analyzed the problems and considered alternatives. Besides, there was an influx of interesting
people. Many West Germans, I explained, had
moved to Leipzig, Dresden, and East Berlin because
they were tired of the status quo and wanted to
take part in a total re-making of society.

The art scene was flourishing, having been freed
from the restrictions of a repressive regime that had
kept it underground for so long. These people had
something to say. They knew that evil was no mere
abstraction. They'd been through the mill, and now
they were making their voices heard. My listeners
were amazed and immediately begged to come for a
visit—they had to see what I was describing with
their own eyes. That was nice. Besides, it was time

for me to go home, too. I needed to get back in
touch with my roots.

As soon as I returned to Germany, I began planning what to show my foreign guests when they
arrived in Leipzig. But, in comparison to southern
France, my hometown suddenly seemed gray and
drab. Surely, this was not the city I'd boasted
about! Or was our picture of the East just something we had conjured up to make everyday life
after the Wall a bit more bearable? Who had we
been kidding?

Truth be told, by the late '90s, many of us began to
give up on the East altogether. There were few opportunities available, and nothing exciting ever
happened. The only options seemed to be to get a
job working for a bank, a local newspaper, an in-
surance company, or the government. Unwilling to
make a complete break, we moved to Berlin—East
Berlin, of course.

While I couldn't deny the attractions of Western
neighborhoods like rough-and-tumble Kreuzberg
or fashionable Savignyplatz, I would never have

considered settling down in one. None of my East German friends lived there—East Germans just didn't move to West Berlin. It was an unwritten law which, if broken, required justification, just like if you smoked an unfashionable brand of cigarettes.

One time, near the end of the decade, I went to visit a West German friend, Jan, on the western side of the Spree River. He lived just across the bridge where the old border crossing had been. Flushed with excitement, I told him how relieved I was that I'd made it across despite the late hour and the fog. Even though the front light on my bicycle didn't work, no one had stopped me to ask what I was doing sneaking into the West or to have me empty the contents of my backpack. I was thrilled. I couldn't believe I'd made my first border crossing by bike. Jan looked at me as if I should get a life.

A couple of weeks later, we went to a soccer game at the Olympic Stadium, deep within West Berlin. While we were waiting for the kick-off, Jan confessed that the whole *Ostscheiß*, or "East bull-shit," as he put it, really got on his nerves. For him, the East-West divide was totally passé. It was boring. Even on the night that the borders had first been opened, he'd have preferred to watch the spectacle on TV rather than live on the streets. Meanwhile, he'd grown tired of the whole thing. Like many West German guys, Jan was sick of discussing the GDR past. What did it have to do with his own life? As far as he could tell, nothing.

It was Jan's idea to go the game. Hertha Berlin was playing Cologne, where Jan was from, and we sat in the visitors' fan block. Lots of people from the Cologne area had recently moved to Berlin. The visitors' section, in any case, was sold-out. Jan had been to almost every Hertha home match, he said, since the team had made it to the first division at the beginning of the 1990s. He liked the club, but its fans were getting far too "eastified" for his taste. To illustrate what he meant, he pointed toward the opposite section where a group of brutish-looking Hertha supporters were unfurling a team flag with skulls and crossbones and trying to attach it to a barrier separating them from the playing field. Jan was right. The place names written on the banners were mostly satellite Eastern suburbs known for their low average income and radical right-wing political leanings.

Jan didn't have to explain why he, despite having lived in Berlin for more than a decade, still rooted for Cologne's perennially mediocre team—it was natural, Cologne was his home team. No one thinks it's strange for people to be attached to their home teams, even if they haven't lived at "home" in years. Yet, these are the same people who, when it comes to East German history, think the past has nothing to do with their present lives.

It's only now, in the second decade after the opening of the Wall, that we've truly arrived in Berlin. You sense that the place will start to settle down in the next ten years, that the worst is over. We've grown attached to spots in both the East and the West—the concourses of Frankfurter Allee, the rail yards at Warschauer Brücke, the Prenzlauer Berg planetarium, and Görlitzer Park in Kreuzberg. It's great to be able to play ping pong on trendy Eastern squares like Helmholtzplatz; or to while away the evenings in the beer garden at the revitalized Prater Theater; or to watch the sun set over Mauerpark, or "Wall Park," which no longer stands in the Wall's shadow. We talk of love by day on the steps of Sanssouci Castle, and go to the Volksbühne at night to see plays by Frank Castorf or listen to our favorite radio host Jürgen Kuttner. We may not feel at home at the Arkonaplatz flea market or snobby bars like Rheingold but, on Sundays, we can make afternoon excursions to West Berlin to explore the districts of Schöneberg and Friedenau or to lie around on the banks of Lake Nikolas. Nice places to live, we say to each other before taking the subway back home to East Berlin.

Today's borders no longer follow the lines where the Wall once stood. Instead everyone has their own personal ones. The Dussmann franchise's gigantic music and book shop, the Galeries Lafayette department store, or Borchardt's restaurant may lie geographically within East Berlin, but they aren't part of my world. Friends who live on Savignyplatz in the West sometimes confess that they don't even know where Friedrichshain is, although it's long been regarded as *the* up-and-coming Eastern district. "Someday," they say, "we'll have to go and have a look for ourselves." It doesn't matter; they can stay at home, if they want. We can always take the subway over to the West, if we feel like seeing them.

Although I've gotten used to the city, Berlin has never become a true home. Friends of mine who were born in East Berlin often complain that they no longer recognize the place. They long for the familiar courtyards, the old-fashioned bakeries, and the crumbling, pre-renovated buildings. They despise nouveau-riche yuppie playgrounds like Auguststraße and the Hackesche Höfe—that's where *they* used to play. I know what they mean; all I have to do is think of Leipzig. Just like me, my friends have been forced to assimilate into a foreign culture that's grown up on their native soil, a culture that constantly requires them to exchange the old for the new.

## 3. The Ugly Years:

*On Our Battles with Bad Taste*

Christmas was a pretty bizarre holiday in the East Germany of the 1990s. On the afternoon of the 24th, before the family even had decorated the tree, there'd be great big plastic shopping bags all over the place, which announced—none too subtly— where Mom and Dad had bought the gifts. From the bags, we knew that our parents had again done their one-stop holiday shopping at Globus, a discount retailer whose wares are divided into three categories: food, non-food, and textiles. Such temples of bad taste sprouted up everywhere in the 1990s, and our parents couldn't get enough of them. Why change your shopping habits just because it was Christmas?

What gift you were given depended on what was on sale the day they were there. One year, for example, there might be four crates of mandarins and oranges, two bags of nuts, two packs of Melitta premium coffee, four bars of Sarotti chocolate, and a couple of bottles of sickly sweet Rotkäppchen sparkling wine. We mixed the wine into a weak Christmas punch and drank it with the ten kilos of baked goods from Riesa, a town on the Polish border—our parents' nod to native industry.

The colorful spectrum of products available in the free-market economy was, frankly, too much for many East Germans. The older generation, especially, developed an iron-clad set of principles that it hoped would ensure safe shopping. One of the most obvious tenets was quantity over quality. Chocolates ideally came in ping-pong-table-sized boxes, and we could already see that we would still be finishing off the last of the Christmas gingerbread next summer at the beach.

The high point of the afternoon came once the first bottle of Rotkäppchen was opened. Someone would make a toast, and we would all wish each other a Merry Christmas. I knew from experience that the others would all drain their glasses and the bottle would soon be empty. What they didn't know was that I'd poured my glass down the sink and hidden the remaining bottles of the God-awful stuff in the basement—as I'd done last year.

Sometimes our parents would try to come up

with a surprise. They would splurge for reusable cotton shopping sacks instead of throw-away plastic bags. The name of the supermarket was printed on the sacks, and you could buy them at check-out counter. Our parents would place them atop the gifts like a crowning achievement. I would stand in front of my pile of presents and wish that I were somewhere far away. It wasn't even three o'clock in the afternoon yet.

I was truly shocked at how my parents' taste developed during those years. Back in the GDR, things weren't so bad. When I thumbed through their wedding albums with my friends, my parents actually looked trendy for their day. Or at least normal. My father wore white shirts with rolled-up sleeves and hip-hugger jeans. His hair was long and hung over his forehead and ears. My mother went for short skirts with knee-high boots, fur-collared jackets, and vertically striped sweaters with silver threading. There was nothing in the photos that I wouldn't have worn myself, nothing to be ashamed of.

Christmas was a more tasteful endeavor, too. When we were little—right after summer vacation, as we were still memorizing our new fall school schedules—our parents would start exploiting their connections to procure our Christmas necessities. What made Christmas Christmas were the specialty items my folks could get only with great difficulty— Hungarian salami, pork roast, oranges, nuts, pearl onions, *boeuf à la mode* with asparagus tips, artificial peanut-flavored snacks from Czechoslovakia, and western chocolate for the kids. If a family didn't have relatives on the other side of the Wall, they'd go to the black market.

People who never have had the pleasure of shopping in East German stores may have difficulty imagining what our stores were like. They weren't empty, but they only had one type of any given product: one kind of butter, one flavor of jam, one brand of soft drink. Because there were so few choices, our parents knew what was good and what wasn't; they were intimately familiar with the few brands that existed in the GDR.

What was it about the '90s that so unbalanced their sense of taste? After 1989, the stores were flooded with all kinds of stuff. East Germans were not able to distinguish between the many goods and brands. We couldn't tell the difference between Danish and Irish, salted and unsalted, full-cream and low-fat butter. It was overwhelming. Besides, back in the GDR, we did not use consumer goods to define us as individuals. That's why, after the Wall, our parents were so befuddled when they went shopping in well-stocked Western department stores.

Why couldn't they get it through their heads that a package of *kaffee* (Western coffee)—however many doors it may have opened back in the GDR—wasn't going to impress anyone? That they no longer had to leave offerings on bureaucrats' desks; and that we kids didn't have to deliver bribes to

This ad for West German coffee (*kaffee*) promises East Germans that (with their low prices) "The Revolution Continues."

strangers anymore? Western consumer goods had been the secret currency in the German Democratic Republic. Western chocolates, coffee, or electrical appliances were the keys that could open locked doors. Construction materials, home fixtures like bathtubs, heating units, or sinks were particularly rare and valuable commodities and, thus, in permanent demand, as were car parts, luxury foods, and vacation spots on the water

Official propaganda notwithstanding, the GDR had been a materialistic society, in which everyone constructed his own little personal image with help of status symbols. Even as children, we were able to tell the difference between Eastern and Western jeans. We knew an Eastern "Germania" skateboard was a cheap copy of the Adidas one. We secretly licked the pink erasers from the West, which were rumored to be fruit-flavored, and we hoarded empty Pelikan ink cartridges, which always rattled so pleasantly in your fountain pen. We wouldn't have traded them for a whole truckload of full ones of the Eastern Heiko brand. Likewise, it was a major source of embarrassment if your aha or Modern Talking stickers came from Poland, and not from Western teen magazines like *Pop Rocky* and *Bravo*.

Back in the GDR, everyone dreamed of premium

Czechoslovakian beer and saved up for a color television or a Lada car. The repository for many of these treasures was the family summer cottage or *dacha*. On weekends, the family would go to work on the dacha until everything—down to the toilet scrub brush—was wood paneled. Our dachas were like tiny villas, outfitted with a range of conveniences—hammocks, plastic swimming pools, jungle gyms, coffee machines, refrigerators, fitted living-room furniture, and color TVs. And no dacha was complete without velour wallpaper. As a kid, I used to run my hands

Kitchens in one of East Germany's new housing developments. They all looked the same—tiny, no windows, and full of kitschy junk.

over it, against the grain, until my palms itched and were covered with red spots.

After the Wall, our parents seemed overwhelmed by the sheer variety of goods available in every store. Or perhaps they simply gave up trying to distinguish worthwhile stuff from junk once the challenge of the hunt was gone. Before, they'd gone on veritable expeditions to satisfy their tiniest material wants. Now, the game was over and they had lost.

We kids swung in the opposite direction. We became obsessed with acquiring all the right status symbols. In the run-up to our parents' birthdays, we would feverishly debate what to give them. We could never agree, and instead searched forever for the perfect gift idea. We did not realize how much we'd already surrendered to the fine distinctions of Western consumerism, and how that had created distance between us and our parents. We envisioned the perfect holiday party—our parents, surrounded by friends and family, sitting behind a mound of presents in the local restaurant or in somebody's backyard. In our imaginations our fathers always got tasteful gifts—a bottle of liquor or cologne; perhaps also a book about World War II, one of those newsstand paperbacks with titles like *Field Marshal Rommel in Africa;* and shirts, pajamas, and underwear. Our mothers always got bubble bath with matching body lotion, bottles of wine, tablecloths, or pepper crackers.

In reality, our presents were always small, expensive, and wrapped in what we considered stylish paper. The other birthday guests would look on in horror as we presented our gifts. Our mothers or fathers would quickly unwrap them, say a polite thank-you, and then toss them on the pile with the other presents, as though trying to hide our gifts from view. You could see they thought what we'd bought was an unnecessary and inappropriate waste of money.

Sometimes, it seems as though we, the children of reunification, purposely sought out these uncomfortable situations. As though we were trying to show everyone that we'd put the East behind us and that we knew what true style was. We studiously ignored the fact that the GDR was still a thing of the recent past, and that those who lived there were struggling to find their way in what they called "the changing times." Our parents seemed afraid that we kids might accuse them of hypocrisy, should they choose to "go West German" and betray the values of the Socialist society in which they raised us. In fact, that was precisely what our gifts were encouraging them to do.

Gradually I came to admit that a Mont Blanc fountain pen probably wasn't much use to people who shuffled from one state-created job to the next, dealing with juvenile delinquents or pruning trees in parks. Or who were sent to vocational school to learn how to use a Macintosh computer or to draw engineering drafts for airplanes. We were going to have to give up our absurd expectations. If only, as I used to joke, because we too might be at vocational school in the not-too-distant future. Remarks like these didn't do very much to lighten the mood. The long and short of it was: We could never find the right presents for our parents because Eastern Germany after the Wall had remained a pragmatic society, still oriented toward things that had practical uses, rather than things that were supposed to demonstrate one's good taste or fashion sense. The older generation didn't get this shift; so pretty soon we gave up exchanging gifts at all.

The irony was that we, ourselves, initially had a hard time mastering the finer points of Western consumerism. During the mid-1990s, East Germany was getting a healthy boost in population from people coming in from the West. When I was a student in Leipzig, one of my new neighbors was Jonathan from Hamburg. Jonathan received regular care packages from his mother and, in the spirit of communalism, he used to share his PC goodies—fair-trade coffee, handmade candles, and raisin-and-date cookies—with me. I never dared help myself to more than one or two pieces of his health-food chocolate, made with unprocessed sugar and genuine cocoa. It seemed too good to eat while watching TV or shooting the breeze.

Jonathan was proud of his non-renovated apartment with its coal heating and shared toilet, but when he invited me to dinner, there was always steamed fennel with cream sauce, whole-grain bread, and Bordeaux or Beaujolais. My fork trembled in my hand. He would talk about how "authentic" the overweight milk ladies were in their white aprons; about how to best light a coal oven; and about how he had learned to appreciate East European dishes like soljanka and goulash. It was all so quaint! Meanwhile, I tried to memorize the vegetables on my plate, so that I would recognize them at my corner market and be able to ask for them by name.

Jonathan's apartment was Spartan, admirably low-key, and random in its organization. GDR apartments were always crammed with furniture. Our new neighbors from the West, by contrast, usually had self-consciously simple things—a rustic desk in front of the window, its surface covered with a computer and thousands of notes, papers, and folders. In the corner of the room, there'd be a mattress on the floor. Photos, dried flowers, postcards, and cutout newspaper articles hung on the otherwise bare walls. The stereo was always on the floor, and with every step, you'd stumble over paperbacks, empty CD cases, photos, and comic books. Then there was the obligatory ceiling work. Jonathan was particularly proud of his. He'd painstakingly cleaned the ornate molding work with a toothbrush and then painted it over in fleshy pastels to achieve the impression of patina.

When we went shopping together at lunchtime, Jonathan would buy a couple of apples and ask the dumbfounded supermarket clerk whether the tomatoes were "native produce." He never used plastic bags for fruit and vegetables, and he always apologized profusely for his Müller's blood-orange juice

Interior decorating
wasn't exactly a great
strength in the GDR.

drink because it didn't come in recyclable packaging. When I'd put my chocolate cookies and Coke down next to his purchases on the check-out conveyer belt, he'd stare in horror. "You'd think the Wall had only come down yesterday," he'd say.

Now that we're older, and people can no longer tell at a glance that we come from the East, I sometimes pause to watch kids from East Berlin, Dresden, or Rostock horsing around on their way home from school. Their sense of fashion is so unerring it makes me shudder, and I can't help thinking back enviously to my own childhood. Did they buy their Nike baseball caps and H&M tops by themselves, or did their parents choose their clothes for them? They're so young, and they already look like real Westerners. How did they do it?

I got my first pair of acid-washed jeans just after the Wall fell and long after they had gone out of style. They were hand-me-downs from my mother, who must have got them when my Dad visited one of the exclusive shops set up by the GDR to relieve West Germans in transit to Berlin of some of their hard currency. The jeans might not have been the latest thing, but I wore them with pride, and to pep them up, I sewed two brightly colored shoelaces, one orange and the other green, to the outer seams. An old friend later told me that he earned a living in the GDR selling colored shoelaces. He'd buy white ones by the carton and then take them home and dye them with food coloring in great big pots on his stove. He always had hundreds of them hanging out to dry in his tiny apartment. It must have looked as though it were raining colored threads.

Back then, our mothers did everything they could to see that we were properly dressed. Hand-me-downs from the West were shared not just be-

Back in the GDR, these sneakers were called "Five-Mark-Shoes" because they had no brand name and they cost five marks. Everybody knew them because everybody wore them. They've since achieved cult status.

tween family members but with neighbors and coworkers as well. Week in, week out, our mothers scoured the stores, not to buy what was necessary, but to see what was possible. They knitted us homemade sweatshirts—we called them "sweet shirts"—and hand stenciled them with brand names and images we'd selected from out-of-date Western catalogues. The admiration of our classmates at school was almost guaranteed.

There are pictures from a certain period of my childhood when the sweatshirts and sweatpants had just replaced the track suit. We look so insecure in those pictures. Hesitant, somewhat spooked, and always inappropriately dressed, we stare straight into the camera. You can see in our eyes that we only want to do things right, and that we lack the necessary knowledge and skills. When I look at us standing there awkwardly in our homemade fashions, I feel a swell of emotion. All the embarrassment comes back, the shame we used to feel when, on holidays in Hungary and Bulgaria, we'd run across well-dressed West Germans, Britons, Belgians, or Dutch and wish that someday, somehow, we would look exactly like them. In the weeks after the Wall fell, we'd drive across the border to Hertie and Woolworth's and buy a bunch of junk with our welcome money.

Perhaps, someday, when I tell my own children about what it was like for me growing up, I'll just pretend that I was born in 1997 at the age of twenty-one—that I simply erased the uncertain, ugly years from my life. I already feel the intense desire to destroy all this photographic evidence of our tenuous apprenticeship in the finer points of fashion. By the mid-'90s, we'd been part of the West for five years, but we still didn't know how to dress properly. There was no mistaking where we were from—we just couldn't get it right.

The problem wasn't lack of effort. In the first years after reunification I spent every spare minute I had studying the West, analyzing what I saw and trying to understand. The goal was the perfect copy. I didn't want to stick out anymore. I was tired of people in the supermarket making snide comments about my clothes, tired of going to restaurants and not recognizing half of what was on the menu. I wanted know everything everyone else knew. My brain was a perpetual scanner, registering the body language, the behavior, the slang, the haircuts, and the wardrobes of my fellow citizens from the West.

Who was East and who was West? University was an ideal place to play this guessing game, and with a bit of practice, I felt I had it down. Women were easier to pinpoint than men: Western women displayed a clear sense of ease when dealing with brand-name fashions. In a gesture of understatement, they would combine designer names with things they'd picked up in second-hand shops or run-of-the-mill department stores. It was how they showed that they'd kept their feet on the ground. Part of their secret was not to be too dependent on trends of the moment. They wore this or that sweater, for instance, sometimes precisely because it had gone out of style. In my case, I was sure, that would be taken as a sign of cluelessness.

The West German woman of the 1990s was idiosyncratic but, to my astonishment, she never seemed to make a wrong move. She would scan through a national newspaper in the last five minutes before a lecture, chic and self-assured, while her East German sister read her hometown rag, stuffed her face with a homemade sandwich, and looked nervously about the lecture hall. The West German woman remained absorbed in her paper, as if it were beneath her dignity to honor anyone else with a glance.

The East German woman of the early '90s favored a potpourri of clothing manufacturers that fell short of qualifying as brand-name designers. She meandered when shopping and was easily distracted by advertisements. She was permanently on the lookout for novelty. Always buying panties and T-shirts at the same store seemed monotonous. Why immediately sacrifice a bit of hard-won freedom? Hadn't she just learned that there was more to fashion than just wearing what everybody else did? The East German woman favored square, high-heeled, fur-lined boots from chain stores like Deichmann or Reno. She still sported blouses under her sweater, preferably tucked into her jeans. Brightly colored knitwear was perennially en vogue. As far as hairstyles were concerned, though, the East German woman was a model of consistency. How could something that had served you well since puberty suddenly go out of fashion?

It was more difficult to distinguish origin within groups that were defined by a specific uniform. There was no telling East from West with hippies, and female law students from Dresden quickly adopted the pink blouse and Benetton sweater worn by their peers from Hamburg. The would-be models, who seemed to float into morning lecture halls directly from the front pages of fashion magazines, were likewise difficult to place. It required a lot of practice and thorough knowledge of *Elle* and *Vogue* to determine where trendiness had degenerated into a kind of shallow uniformity. In time, I stopped playing this game. By the end of the '90s, at least in the German capital, it had become impossible to differentiate native and non-native Berliners, or East and West Germans, by the way they dressed. Most of my guesses turned out to be wrong.

What did people think when they saw me? In the later years of the decade, more and more people thought I came from the West. I had learned my lessons and could no longer be easily unmasked. I had long since begun to combine brand names with cheaper things to show that I had kept my feet on the ground. I now bought my shoes from small boutiques and had my hair styled. I lost my Saxon accent; no one could detect it in my speech anymore.

## After the Wall

But, strangely enough, every time someone thought I was from the West—from Hamburg or Nuremberg—I felt sad.

At the same time, if someone had said they could tell at a glance that I was from the East, I would have doubled over and started bawling. That didn't happen, thank God. One of my old friends, who had studied diction as part of his actors' training, did point out a few residual traces of Saxony in the way I spoke. It was nothing much, just a couple of slushy endings to words on my answering machine message, but Saxon was considered among the ugliest and most provincial accents in Germany. I got rid of the problem by re-recording my message. I wasn't going to let an answering machine spoil my connection with the West.

# 4. Role Reversals:

## On Dealing with Our Parents

Our new West German university friends had a lot of funny ideas about intergenerational relationships. They tended toward over-exuberant gestures of friendship, staging eccentrically ambitious family get-togethers and then gleefully letting different worlds collide. Their parents were their friends, who'd stuck by them through thick and thin. Every time our West German peers had relationship problems or failed an exam, they'd call their folks, pour their hearts out on the phone, and then catch the next train back home. They'd stay there until their egos had recovered, spending most of their time on their parents' couches, and only returning to us and life in the big city once they'd made a complete recovery.

There was nothing better than Mommy's advice, they confided, when you got in a jam. She had been through it all. She spoke from experience and was always up for a heart-to-heart chat at 3:30 A.M. As for Dad, he earned the money, helped the kids move, negotiated their rent with the landlord, put up bookshelves, and did their taxes.

When our parents called us to say they were coming to visit, our West German friends would always suggest going out as a group to eat or to see a play. It was the perfect opportunity to get to know one another. We children of the GDR, they insisted, should stop pretending we had emerged from a void. We weren't orphans, after all.

We liked our West German friends, but it was really irritating how they dragged their parents along everywhere, bringing them to our favorite bars, touring the lecture halls and the university cafeteria, meandering through the flea market arm in arm with their mothers, like young couples in love. And now, here they were suggesting that we do the same. Not on your life.

Such an enterprise would end in complete disaster. Our parents weren't like theirs. Of course we went out with them to dinner or to the theater when they came to visit—but we did it alone. We preferred to keep our parents sheltered. They hadn't been through anything like our lives. They didn't speak from experience. We called *other* people when we had problems at three-thirty in the morning.

We'd had ample experience with West German parents over the course of the '90s, and our encounters with them had been the stuff of constant, heated discussion. I was always a bit jealous when my friend Jenny, who dated Jonathan for a while during the mid-1990s, would rave ecstatically about his parents' silver-gray Volvo. The car was just so "subtle," she would repeat, over and over, as if that were something I wouldn't be able to understand. Sometimes, when Jonathan's parents were visiting, they'd let her take the thing out for a solo spin. She'd tell me all about it later. She'd light a cigarette and pantomime putting the automatic in gear and cruising around, her elbow lolling out the driver's side window, the butt dangling from the corner of her mouth. Just imagine that, she would say. An East German behind the wheel of a Volvo with Hamburg plates.

Dinners with Jonathan's family, at least as Jenny described them, always followed the same pattern. His parents would take their time catching up on the latest news, showing exaggerated enthusiasm for such and such aspect of their son's life; then the conversation would turn to a standard repertoire of topics. How great things looked in the East, Jonathan's parents would say, as if to praise Jenny. The improvements were evident before you even left the Autobahn. The potholes were gone; so, too, were those unattractive sausage and beer kiosks on the sidewalks. They could still remember what it was like the last time they had come for a visit. Everything used to stink of coal, the fumes from the old East German cars had clogged the air, and you couldn't find a decent Italian restaurant anywhere. Leipzig was hardly recognizable. Everything had turned out just fine, Jonathan's father would sigh, adding that he didn't mind paying extra taxes as long as you could see the improvements.

Jenny knew what was expected of her, as the East German girlfriend, in such discussions. She would sit up straight in her chair, put on a proud expression and smile at Jonathan's father with ex-Communist gratitude in her eyes. At that point, Jonathan's mother would take over, steering the conversation from the fabulous theater scene in East Germany to the plethora of opportunities now available to young people. Happiness was of your own making—you just had to be in the right place at the right time. Jenny would sense that her boyfriend's parents were now inviting her to speak her mind, to tell them how she and her East German friends had used the chance that history had given them to put the Communist past behind them and to make something of their lives. As she began to relate how her life had changed in the past few years, Jonathan's parents would sit up a bit straighter in their chairs, eyes gleaming with patriotism. Their euphoria was impossible to resist. It would wash over them, taking Jenny and Jonathan in its wake. Everyone at the table was filled with self-contentment.

By contrast, we Easterners could never help feeling a bit frustrated when we had to deal with our parents. Because we kept them hidden away, there were no evenings with them and our West German friends, but if there had been, the mood would hardly have been one of patriotically inflected mutual glee. And taking your boyfriend along was a big mistake. Jenny and I knew that no occasion, however celebratory, could prevent our parents from engaging in one of their typical monologues.

East German parents' speeches always began with the blanket statement that a lot had changed for the better and that, of course, there was no comparing the Federal Republic of Germany with the GDR. For decades they'd wanted nothing more than to see Italy or Paris with their own eyes, and now they'd been able to realize their life-long dreams of buying a house of their own in that new development on the outskirts of town.

"We've been very lucky, really," my parents would say. A friend of theirs worked for a home repairs company so they'd gotten the bathroom fixtures and tiles at cost. They'd done a lot of the work themselves in their spare time. More and more people were moving into the development. The roads were now paved, and street signs were being put up everywhere. Especially pleasing was the man-made lake at the old mine, which was beginning to fill with water. No sir, our parents would say with a smile, they had no reason to complain, but. . . .

There was always a "but." It was a bit of a shame, Jenny's father would say softly after a brief pause, that her mother, who had earned a steady income as a book illustrator, was now out of a job and had no prospects of finding work. As if to gather his strength, he would reach for his glass of beer and take a gulp, before setting it audibly—too audibly Jonathan would have said—back on the table. Jenny knew that this was a signal. The tirade was about to start.

Things were great today, he would continue—for young people. People from the older generation were happy that their children could now go to university anywhere in the world. They themselves had traveled to London to inspect the campus and the lecture halls. They couldn't be more pleased if their children took advantage of all the new opportunities. But, today's times weren't for them. Those on the other side of the Wall didn't understand anything. (At this point Jenny's parents would lean over toward Jonathan.) And to be honest, if they had known what was coming, they might have stayed home on Monday evenings in the Fall of 1989. They hadn't marched through the streets for the way things were now.

Having been raised to be polite, our West German boyfriends would rack their brains for a way out of this uncomfortable conversation. They might decide on an offensive tact. They would try to win our parents over with arguments, analysis, and explanations. It was all in vain. We knew our parents, so we knew that no amount of analyzing and explaining was going to help. We had been through too many of these "discussions"—they always started calmly and always ended with our parents cursing everything new and defending everything old. That was their life. Explanations did no good; explanations didn't get them jobs.

That's why there were important rules to be followed at home during dinner table discussions. We weren't allowed to interrupt our parents' monologues, raise objections, or ask rhetorical questions. It wasn't just that they would think we were trying to show them how superior and Western we were or how well we, in contrast to them, understood the new system. Oh no, *they saw through* what they contemptuously dismissed as "conditions today." Scarcely pausing for breath, they would lecture us about unemployment, social anonymity, political corruption, economic hardship, and so on.

In our parents' view, children weren't supposed to know as much as their parents—so we kept the things we had experienced, and they hadn't, carefully concealed from them. Jenny didn't mention that she'd been out to dinner with Jonathan's parents. She didn't tell her parents that she had failed an exam, that her job was more important to her than a university degree, or that people nowadays neither got married at twenty-two nor finished their studies at twenty-four. Our parents had no idea how much our apartments cost or how much we had paid for the rental truck when we moved. They didn't know we had voted for the Democratic Socialist Party, the successor to the old Eastern-

German Communist one, because we found its acid-tongued spokesman so amusing. They had no clue how much we had spent on our last Italian holiday. We protected them from our lives and protected our lives from them.

The fall of the Wall had transformed each of us into something akin to a child prodigy, upon whom great expectations were placed. There was not much for older East Germans to be proud of. The GDR had lost to the West, and now all East Germans were expected to assimilate into West German society. That, in turn, was viewed as a kind of collective upward social mobility, and we, the children of the first "immigrants," were expected to achieve that goal. We had come from nowhere, and now everyone expected great things. At least, that's what people whispered in our ears. To achieve this greatness, our gazes had to be directed ahead and not behind. It was crucial for us to forget our roots as quickly as possible. We had to become flexible, adaptable. It made no difference whether we came from a family of painters, plumbers, photographers, dentists, or teachers. We were the sons and daughters of history's losers—mocked by the victors as proletarians, people to whom totalitarian conformity and the reputation for laziness clung like a bad odor.

## After the Wall

The real truth about East Germany was to be kept
to ourselves. We never admitted to our parents that
the ugliness and banality of the East depressed us;
or that we found it absurdly pompous for Dresden
or Leipzig to behave as though they were major
world metropolises. We never said that we found
the new cadre of politicians in the East, by turns,
ridiculous, self-righteous, odious, suspect, or simply unbelievably bland. We never told them how
sick we were of our countrymen—the stupid skin-
heads on the Baltic coast who lined up in pseudo-
military rows outside their tents; the old men in the
supermarket who ordered us to get a shopping bas-
ket, if we wanted to buy something; the old ladies
who complained that our cars were blocking the entrance to the laundromat. If we rode our bikes on
the sidewalk, cane-brandishing retirees would leap
out in front of us, sending us flying over the handlebars when we jammed on the brakes. It was all
so provincial, so small-minded.

Our parents knew nothing of this. Conversations
with them weren't exactly the best forum for us to
come out of the closet as East-West hermaphrodites.
At home we spoke with Eastern accents, relearning
them, if necessary, for the occasion. No matter how
much effort we had exerted trying to speak like

everybody else, the East wasn't going to let our generation off easy. And talking back wasn't an option.

Jonathan, of course, couldn't understand why we couldn't discuss things with our parents. Occasionally he would suggest that Jenny simply try to have a constructive chat with her folks about her problems at university and the way she wanted to live her life. Jenny's face would go pale, and she'd briefly consider whether to admit that she wasn't really certain whether her parents even knew what she was studying. But then, she would look into her boyfriend's eyes and decide that it was probably better to say nothing at all.

Jonathan was of the opinion that our problems with our parents were a typical generational conflict, part and parcel of the changing times, which could be solved if all concerned agreed to compromise. He said that everyone, sooner or later, had to leave the nest. He'd been through it himself when he moved from Hamburg to Berlin.

Jenny wasn't sure whether he really understood what we were talking about, and it irritated her that Jonathan would always look at her out of the corner of his eye when giving this advice, as though realizing for the first time that his girlfriend was from the

GDR. As though he were wondering whether she might not be exactly like her parents.

I tried to picture Jonathan at home—having constructive discussions with his parents—and every time I did so I'd mentally stretch out the word "constructive" as through pulling it apart from both ends in my fingers. Jonathan's family probably solved the newspaper crossword puzzle together before sitting down to eat. Then they'd debate the problems in the Third World and the federal budget deficit, and argue, democratically, about who would drive out on the weekend and buy next week's non-pasteurized cheese from the farmers in Schleswig-Holstein.

We East Germans couldn't afford to engage in "constructive" generational conflict. We didn't have the luxury of rebelling against our parents. Their generation was depressed and defeated enough as it was, and we, who had been lucky enough to have been born relatively late in the life of the GDR, didn't want to kick people who were already down. The fall of the Wall had already destroyed all our parents' illusions. They had nothing important left for us to undermine.

And who were we to say that, in their places, we would have done things any differently—that we wouldn't have collaborated with the Secret Police or joined the Party? Would we really have distributed political flyers, published an underground news-paper, or absconded to the West? The German Democratic Republic already had consigned itself to the ashcan of history before we even had to face such questions.

It would have been presumptuous of us to pass judgment on our parents. So we had no option other than to join them in a pact of mutual non-aggression. God knows, there'd been enough dis-tance between us and our parents in the past, and there was sure to be more in the future.

Our common history ended the day the Wall came down. After that, they'd spent their time worrying about their jobs, while we memorized the organizational structures of the West German parlia-ment, the lyrics to the national anthem, and the facts surrounding the 1953 popular uprising against the Communist regime. Their marriages failed, while we tried to decide whether to spend our year abroad in the United States during high school or to wait until after we had started university. They cursed their new West German bosses while we flirted in lecture halls with our peers from Lübeck or Ingolstadt. Now, we had nothing in common. They said very little about their lives, and we said nothing at all about ours. Their experience had become obsolete—at least for us. There was no advice they could give us.

And that's why none of us even dreamed of inviting West German friends to go out with us and our parents. Our family bonds were too tenuous—they consisted of some sympathy and a large quantity of pity. We didn't attack our parents. We didn't ask what they had done in the past. We tried to defend them, the way you do when your little brother is teased by bullies at school.

Which didn't mean we spent much time with them. That was the biggest change. In the old days, we used any excuse to throw a party and everyone in the family was invited. When I think back on family occasions from my childhood, I remember everyone celebrating deep into the night. Around 10 P.M., the host would take the first liquor bottles from the cabinet and would pour the artificially flavored peanut snacks into the fancy glass bowl he had brought back from Prague. Our mothers drank sparkling wine. We children were allowed eggnog, served in chocolate-dipped sugar cones. One of our fathers would clear his throat. The toast was always dead serious, as if the speaker were about to announce the start of a minor revolution. He'd complain about the status quo, about what the Communists were doing to us and to our entire country. The toastmaster's wife would glance nervously around the room and put her index finger to her lips, and we children realized that the time had come to listen up.

The toastmaster had an easy crowd. The guests would quickly second his opinion that everything was better in the West, and that things would be a lot different if people here had the same opportunities as the people over there; if people only had the chance to take charge of their own lives.

Then someone else's father would stand up and tell a couple of jokes about Erich Honecker or Gorbachev. We children, tongues still dipped in eggnog, would prick up our ears and try to memorize what was said, so that we could retell the jokes during Monday morning recess. That was only way to trump the other kids, who had seen the Western television programs that we had missed.

After that, we were sent to bed with alcohol-infused kisses.


Now we only see our parents every other birthday, on important anniversaries, or when someone's child is baptized. When we go back to visit them today, it feels like we're picking them up from an old-age home. That's how remote they are from everyday life as we know it. It's as though we take them out for a short walk, go for an ice cream in a parlor they remember from when they too led active lives, and then re-deposit them in institutional care when the afternoon is over.

The normal parent-child relationship has been inverted. We long for the days when we'll earn our own money, not because we want to free ourselves from our parents' expectations, but because that's how our parents measure success in what they describe as "today's day and age." It's embarrassing to see how they, a few years short of normal retirement age, earn just enough money every month to cover the basic costs of living—like young adults just starting out in their careers. The demise of the GDR has set them back more than twenty years in their working lives.

It's painful to watch them struggle with their new situation. They're like hamsters running around in wheels. Unaware that they can drive themselves as fast or as slow as they like, they spin themselves round and round in circles for fear that the wheel could come to a permanent halt. They purchase a computer so they can surf the Web from home. They enroll in English lessons. What for? Nobody knows. They just think that's what everybody is supposed to do in "today's day and age." We wish they could have the comfort—the stasis—that characterizes the part of Germany we're not from. We pine for the timeless tedium that settles over people's lives in the West like a fog, enveloping everything, leaving no ruptures or open seams.

Our parents are just too old and tired for these times. They're the demoted pupils of another epoch—lost, confused, angry, and frustrated. While we don't pass judgment on them, can anyone blame us for feeling superior? After all, we know more than they do.

We have no other option than to be successful. We want to earn money and show everyone how well we've learned to play the game in the West. If we each make our way and get good jobs in the next ten years, then our parents will have the retrospective satisfaction of not having done everything wrong. If we fail, we'll be one more piece of evidence that the Western system is impenetrable— that no one ever gets ahead without connections. But that possibility is one more thing we don't talk about.

## 5. Give Us This Day Our Daily Pledge:

### On Our Education

Doing good deeds was the main theme of my generation's formative years. We were inspired by the first lines of the official Young Pioneers' song, which could be roughly translated as: "Take your hands from your pockets/ Do some good, don't try to stop it." So we offered our seats in trams to the old and frail, volunteered to carry their coal up from the cellar, and schlepped their shopping bags home for them. On Saturdays, we got up early to perform our *subbotnik*, or our state-encouraged volunteer work, painting the school benches and windowsills and performing other menial tasks. We sold flowers from our school garden in front of the supermarket and donated the proceeds to help Napalm victims in Vietnam. We picked up old milk cartons from the side of the road and helped trim the public hedges in our neighborhood. To honor the working classes on May 1, International

**Stackable plastic bins used in milk deliveries. They stank of sour milk.**

Workers' Day, we folded red carnations from crepe paper or helped weaker pupils with their math homework.

There were lots of official functions available to GDR children, and we were always prepared to take on responsibility. We had important roles to play. The editor of the school paper, the so-called *Agitator,* wrote articles on the joint Soviet-GDR construction of a natural gas pipeline, or read the highlights from the previous night's news programs to the lower classes from a pretend television set made of a cardboard box. The class scribe—always the girl with the best penmanship—wrote up extended protocols of the Young Pioneers' latest afternoon meeting for the group scrapbook. The brigade director checked that everyone did their homework. The Milk Troop delivered milk and the treasurer collected the money for it.

Our lives were a constant struggle for prizes, everything from level-three swimming certificates to academic excellence awards. We put on our

Young Pioneer caps and scarves and saluted the flag. Until the day when we, like Lenin, would be called to carry out some vital, secret mission, we contented ourselves with carrying potato peels to the recycling bins, memorizing the history of the Socialist Party, and sharing our lunchtime sandwiches with kids who weren't as well-off as we were. I never dog-eared the pages of my schoolbooks and, when I did my math exercises, I always did my best to stay neatly within the blue-ink boxes on the page.

I was determined to be a reliable member of the community. The message was: We were responsible for everything. If children were starving in Africa, I took my toys to school and handed them over to the old ladies who sat in our gymnasium registering the donations. While I knew they would be sold to pay for medication or new toys for the Africans, in truth, I was more obsessed with the possibility of buying them back. Kids being kids, I couldn't wait to take re-possession of my things—and, ideally, my classmates' things as well. Still, I was aware that I was a young citizen of a young nation, and it was my duty to advance the cause of Socialism so that it would—someday in the distant future—achieve the great ideal of a Marxist-Leninist workers' paradise.

## After the Wall

The school monument. We would line up on the left and right, our hands raised in Socialist greeting, while our teachers laid wreaths in honor of war veterans.

I knew I had the good fortune to be born in a time of peace in a Socialist state. War, privation, and hunger were things I only knew secondhand. Still, the clouds of war were always on the horizon in the 1980s. The popular struggle for peace and justice had not yet ended. I had to do my part—if necessary with a gun in my hand—to help contain the imperialist threat. Erich Honecker and other comrades had gone to prison fighting to ensure that war would never again originate from German soil. We had a responsibility to see that their heroic legacy continued. Like the craftsman at his bench, the farmer atop his thresher, and the policeman by the side of the road, we children pledged to become educated and cultured citizens, promising to use the skills and knowledge we learned to help realize the great, humanistic ideals of our society. Each person in the GDR had his own special part in this struggle, and our parents, teachers, older comrades in the Free German Youth, and godfathers from the world of industry would be at our sides, helping us every step of the way.

I would also be responsible for Ronald Reagan's Star Wars missile defense system, at least theoretically, if I didn't faithfully renew my commitment to Socialism and give my absolute all when my class ran through military drills behind the school. In 1985, my Young Pioneers troop buried our scrapbook in the ground so that, if the world hadn't been destroyed by nuclear war in the meantime, the Pioneers of the year 2000 could dig up our records and see that generations of schoolchildren before them had also fought for the just cause. The burial must have broken our class scribe's heart; week after week she'd flawlessly noted all our activities on the pages between the book's black spring-bound covers. I was upset, too. The only consolation was that the book was buried safely for posterity in the landfill behind our housing development.

The entire world was at war. At least that's how I

remember it as a child. Everyone—the Sandinistas, the ANC, the Angolans—seemed to be fighting over something. The GDR was only spared that horrible fate thanks to the resolve of its brothers in the Warsaw Pact, the might of the Soviet military, and the bravery of the GDR's own National People's Army.

We had to beware the imperialists—nuclear war could break out at any moment. After school, I dug bunkers with my friends—our plan was to crawl into them and hide when the bombs started falling. We even set up an early warning system, deciding who would inform whom, should that fateful event come to pass. If there were going to be survivors, we wanted to be among them.

Lying in bed on summer evenings, after enjoying my favorite meal of fried bologna and macaroni, the sky outside my windows would sometimes light up in fiery reds. It was only a sunset, but I couldn't help imagining that the first houses were already on fire. Would I be able to reach our bunker in time? Exhaustion would eventually overcome fear and I would fall asleep, clutching my pillow.

The next morning, I would scribble hasty letters to Erich Honecker, imploring him to do everything he could to convince the Americans to put their bombers in the hangars and leave them there.

A page from our past: "The National People's Army celebrates its founding day on March 1."

Tomorrow, I wrote, we would pledge to collect more old paper. Could he please build a gigantic glass ceiling over the GDR to shield us from the bombs? If anyone could do something like that, Honecker could.

Our parents didn't take the war against imperialism quite as seriously as we kids did. Sometimes they seemed downright apathetic. They made their contributions, of course. Our fathers served on the school board and helped organize replacements for broken bathroom windows, while our mothers baked cookies for Women's Career Day or volunteered to show the Young Pioneers how to make potato prints. But they made no bones about it; these duties were a pain in the ass. They always argued over who would have to go to school for parent-teacher conferences. As soon as a school outing was planned, which required three mothers to volunteer as chaperones, parents would start to get sick and have simultaneous meetings at work or hairdresser appointments. Of course, we were forbidden from mentioning this at school. Our job was to sit there silently until other people's parents were picked to be the chaperones.

We had a lot of practice keeping our mouths shut. Our perennial discussions about the previous night's television programs always came to a quick halt whenever a teacher showed up. Either that, or we switched the topic to East German shows we pretended to have watched, instead of Western favorites like *Dynasty* or *Hart to Hart*.

One thing that our parents never tolerated from us was a lack of cleverness. This involved being good at some things and bad at others. The goal was to function as a member of Socialist society without getting in trouble with the authorities or becoming a rabid Party member who was despised by everyone. Cooperation and distance were equally important. We were expected to recognize that taking on official functions at school could help us get into a university-track high school, yet under no circumstances were we to jeopardize our future by attracting attention to ourselves or by making enemies. You could be as mediocre as you wanted in math or history, as long as you got good grades in the things that really mattered: conduct, orderliness, enthusiasm, and application. Bad grades in those subjects meant that our parents would have to spend a Saturday discussing our upbringing with our teacher. To spare my parents this ordeal, I always sat in the second row and, if possible, next to the class geek.

The first commandment was to always know in advance what others wanted you to be and, by following it, I was able to avoid attracting attention. Getting grades in history that were too good or collecting too many old newspapers would make you look uncool. You didn't pack too many Western chocolate bars into your backpack on school camping trips, just as you only wore your best clothes on holidays and when you went to the theater, never to school. People might start talking about you.

Talk was the enemy. The key was to remain invisible and average. Fathers who joined a soccer club or ran a bar in their free time were just as suspect as families with two cars, four kids, and a non-working mother. We were to avoid other kids who never invited us home or who often seemed to have Western bananas in their lunchboxes. The same went for kids from single-parent households. You never knew where you stood with them. Strange as it may sound, the GDR was basically a petty bourgeois society. All most people wanted were two kids (one boy and one girl), a car, and a weekend cottage.

As good 1980s Socialist preteens, our official attitude toward the West was one of contempt. The so-

ciety on the other side of the Wall was one where
teachers were unfairly sacked for their left-wing
convictions, workers were laid off in droves, land-
lords gouged rent from the tenants, and imperialists
dreamed of a neo-fascist Fourth Reich. At least
that's what we were taught in school—but we
didn't really believe it. On the contrary, we were in-
trigued by Westerners, though we hardly ever saw
them. When we did come into contact with Westerners—for example, during the international
Leipzig Book Fair—we were warned by our teachers not to pick up Western chocolate wrappers from
the streets. We were forbidden from pressing our
noses against the windows of Western cars and beg-
ging foreign visitors for plane ticket stubs, stickers,
bars of Toblerone, and Wrigley's Spearmint or
Hubba Bubba chewing gum. Anyone caught at
school with the most cherished of all Western artifacts, a stolen Mercedes hood ornament, was asking
for a quick trip to the principal's office.

The unintended consequence of our teachers'
prohibitions was to transform West Germany into
a nirvana where friendly adults ran around with
candy and gum in their pockets, handing them out
to children on the streets. When I encountered
Westerners on my way back home from school

during the Book Fair, I would give them a long, friendly smile. Perhaps they would share the treasures in their pockets with me. I didn't beg—that was forbidden—but there were no restrictions on giving people a suggestive grin.


Our primary-school education ended in the eighth grade, usually at the age of thirteen, with a ceremony called the *Jugendweihe*, which was a kind of mass Communist confirmation. By that time, we'd been members of the Free German Youth for six months, and most of the boys had already signed up for one-and-a-half to three years of military service. In four years we would all be allowed to join the Party. The *Jugendweihe* was the high point of our young lives, the point at which we were officially accepted as trained Socialists into the great community of the working classes.

Planning for the ceremony began weeks in advance, and no detail, however minor, was left to chance. In the assembly hall of the People's Street-Cleaning Cooperative or some other similar venue, replete with the obligatory brown velour wallpaper, gray linoleum, and thick red drapes, we'd practice mounting the stage alphabetically in groups of five

Wir laden Sie, liebe Eltern, werte Gäste und Euch, liebe Jugendweiheteilnehmer,
zu der am SONNTAG, dem 2. April 1989, 9.00 Uhr,
im Kultursaal des VEB Stadtreinigung stattfindenden

*Jugendweihefeier*

der 144. Oberschule „Erich Kähn" recht herzlich ein.

FDJ-Grundorganisation                    Schulbereichsausschuß
                                          für Jugendweihe

DIE FESTANSPRACHE HÄLT:
ELFRIEDE RICHTER
Vorsitzende des Kreisvorstandes Leipzig-West des
Freien Deutschen Gewerkschaftsbundes

ES WIRKEN MIT:
Ilona Schloß, Gesang und Rezitationen
Martin Hoepfner, Konzertgitarre
Thomas Prakein, Violine

*Festprogramm*

Einzug der Jugendlichen
Nationalhymne
Sonate a-moll, op. 1 für Violine und Gitarre      Jean Baptiste Loillet de Gant
FESTANSPRACHE – GELÖBNIS
Sonate III aus Cantone di Sonate
für Violine und Gitarre                           Nicolo Paganini
ÜBERREICHUNG DER URKUNDEN UND GESCHENKBÜCHER
Bossa nova                                        Gerald Schwertberger
Werte                                             Eva Strittmatter
Die Kraniche fliegen im Keil                      Text und Musik: Kurt Demmler
Stammbuchverse III                                Eva Strittmatter
Wildvögelein                                      Volkslied
aus „Das Impressum"                               Hermann Kant
Fröhlicher Tanz                                   Bearbeitung: Thomas Heyn
Dank der Jugendlichen
Auszug der Jugendlichen
Änderungen vorbehalten

**The program for a *Jugendweihe*
Socialist confirmation ceremony.**

to accept our *Jugend-weihe* certificates and congratulatory bouquets of flowers. Under the proud eyes of our parents, grandparents, and the entire school faculty, we would pledge to give our all for the noble cause of Socialism, to deepen the bonds of friendships with the Soviet Union and fight for the interests of the international proletariat. In addition to the certificate and the flowers, each of us was given a book entitled *On the Meaning of our Lives*. It summed up our short existence in five general questions: Who am I? What can I do? What do I want? To whom can I be useful? Who needs me?

I loved these books. They initially may have
raised some difficult questions, but they always had
satisfying answers at the ready. Skill and knowledge, a sense of social responsibility and duty, class
loyalty, and a willingness to meet the highest standards in our educational and working lives—those
were the characteristics of a true Socialist. Everyone
could acquire such qualities as long as he or she, in
line with the Marxist-Leninist world view, emanci-
pated him- or herself from the false consciousness
of capitalist exploitation and embraced his or her
working-class identity. As the book went on to
make clear, that even applied to the mentally and
physically handicapped. It was awfully comforting
to a group of gangly, pimply preteens. What did we
know about life?


There was no end to the changes in the first couple
of years after 1989. Suddenly, two-car families became common, and many mothers stayed home instead of working. Indeed, many women had time
enough on their hands to have three or four children—which was uncommon in the GDR at the
time. Instead of carrying a clean handkerchief in my
pocket, I had miniature packs of tissues that you

could simply throw away after you'd blown your nose. We children no longer cared who Lenin was, and we never shared the bananas and Western chocolates we brought to school for lunch. Pelikan fountain-pen cartridges, which were available in every stationery store, lost their value as collectibles. The verb "to pledge" died out, as did the fearful references to Ronald Reagan and his imperialists. Whereas social studies instruction had begun with the division of the GDR into local districts, in history (as it was now called) we memorized the names of the federal German states and their capitals. We were expected to fire them off as quick as a pistol: Rhineland-Pfalz: Hessen, North Rhine-Westphalia: Düsseldorf, and so on.

After we'd memorized the states and their capitals, we moved on to the history of the Federal German Republic after 1945. We learned about the first German chancellor, Konrad Adenauer, and the miraculous boom years under his economics minister Ludwig Erhard; the debates surrounding Germany's re-armament and membership in NATO; the plebiscite in Saarland; the student protests of the 1960s; RAF terrorism in the 1970s; and about the 1982 vote of no confidence by which Helmut Kohl had wrested the office of German chancellor from Helmut Schmidt.

## After the Wall

Once, when we were assigned to write an essay on a topic of our own choosing, I decided to write about the role of farmers in the 1953 anti-Communist uprisings in the GDR. The uprising was a topic close to my heart, and a piece of my own history that had been largely ignored by schools in the GDR, where it was dismissed as an instance of counterrevolutionary agitation instigated by West German agents. My history teacher knew little about this event. Before the fall of the Wall, the curriculum had been confined to the rise of Communism, the history of the international workers' movement, and the triumphs of the Soviet Union. My essay topic sent my teacher to the library to read up on the event so she could teach her students about it later. She frequently postponed answering our questions, instead jotting them down and coming back the following day with the required information. She even photocopied my essay on the farmers for her own reference. We needed each other's help.

Our parents still expected us to be clever, indeed more clever than ever before. The task now was to demonstrate your brilliance to everyone around you, especially the teacher. In the discussions that were held on every street corner and in every classroom (and that I soon came to consider utterly superfluous), we were supposed to show how critically we could think about our environment and how skilled we were in formulating alternatives.

Suddenly, the adults wanted to know what we hadn't liked about our former lives and how we would improve the (in their words) "structures" of our classes, phys ed program, and extracurricular activities, everything right on down to the organization of the school choir. As I now lived in a democracy, I did my best not to mull over opinions too much or for too long before opening my mouth, but rather to shoot from the hip, to criticize, and sometimes even to provoke people.

The split pea soup in the school cafeteria made me want to vomit, I said, and there was never enough chocolate pudding to go around. I complained about the fluoride in the water, the mandatory health examinations, the mandatory visits to factory, the mandatory flag saluting, and all the other ideological exercises. Oh yeah, and I wanted to travel, and I needed some Western money. Otherwise, I was basically satisfied with the way my life had been—but I kept that opinion to myself and kept on criticizing, because that was what they wanted us to do.

We didn't have any experience in democracy. We were going to have to take a closer look at it, before we could reasonably negotiate between public expectations and private thoughts.

Not that we stopped fighting. We had been trained to fight, and now that our struggles no longer took place on practice fields behind our school—but instead on the streets—they seemed more worthwhile than ever. We demonstrated for a shorter school week. We marched for the preservation of the GDR's youth-oriented, alternative radio station. Some even went on a short-lived hunger strike in support of our teachers and professors, whose jobs had come under fire as West German educational authorities tried to purge faculties of Communist ideologues.

As long as we could fight for something, we were happy. We were engaging the authorities in a dialogue, we told ourselves. That was what democracy was all about. Citizens were supposed to use the instruments of democracy and actively lobby for their interests. At least, that's what I'd written on the chalkboard under the approving eyes of my West-

ern teachers. That sounded good, and for a short
time I even believed it.

The high school I went to beginning in 1991 was
not far from the coal mines on Leipzig's southern
perimeter. It's something of a minor miracle that the
state never demolished this prewar facility, which
was once home to the National People's Army and
which later was converted into an academy for uni-
versity-bound pupils.

The slag pit began just where the campus left off.
An overgrown strip of land was all that separated us
from the mines, and we were strictly forbidden
from setting foot there. Our teachers told us there
could be old army ammunition lying around. Sometimes between periods, we would stand at the edge
of this strip of land and try to peer through the
trees and brush to catch a glimpse of the silver surface of the mine's artificial lake.

Two years after the Wall fell, I enrolled in the
school. I had to pass a set of rigorous exams to be
admitted because, as our teachers told us, admis-
sions were now subject to the "laws of the free market economy." That meant that if everyone,
regardless of political leaning, was allowed to go to

university, then individual achievement was the only standard for separating the wheat from the chaff. At least, that's what we thought our teachers meant.

On that first day of high school, we were innocent. Ours was the first class to be taught according to a West German syllabus. We didn't know what everything meant. We were just thrilled with our new status: Here we were, the new elite. We didn't have any West German teachers yet and our East German instructors, who had extraordinary faith in us, were always stressing that things were about to take off and change for the better. In the course of the year, however, it became clear that our teachers, unfamiliar as they were with Western standards, rarely dared give us encouraging smiles or bits of praise—to say nothing of top grades. For our part, we no longer knew how to fulfill their expectations. And so we studied as though our lives depended on it. Not a week went by without some new rules and regulations aimed at increasing the pressure and, with it, the performance of East German students. When we went home on Friday, we were always nervous. We could never be sure whether we still had a chance of getting into university or whether we had somehow misplayed our cards.

The following year, some minister of education somewhere decided that none of us probably deserved to be university bound. At the end of the year, we were all to take a supplementary test to determine whether we were indeed qualified. If you didn't get the arbitrary average grade, you'd be kicked out. We took to the streets to demonstrate. The powers above first reconfirmed the new rule, then revised it, then reinstituted it in its original form, then cancelled the whole thing. The truth was that no one knew what was going on anymore. The East German educational authorities had suddenly become remarkably thin-skinned. We doubted that they would ever be able to close the gap with their Western colleagues, not after the many decades spent living apart.

The wheat did, indeed, get separated from the chaff—but not as our school reformers had

Bookplate from a textbook. When schoolbooks in the West became worn and outdated, they were often donated to students in the East.

intended. Some of us continued studying diligently, and some just stopped. We went to class when we felt like it. When we arrived at school in the morning, the first thing we did was to congregate in someone's dorm room, listen to music, smoke cigarettes, and talk about life. As soon as the bell rang ending the final period, we left. Tests were scheduled weeks, often months, in advance, but we only showed up if we had had the time and inclination the night before to study. If we didn't, there were always make-up exams. We aced those because we knew what was on them. I don't remember why, but we never seemed to have a problem getting excused. We probably just signed our sick notes ourselves.

Having renounced all forms of overt rebellion at home, we needed enemies—and those were our teachers. It was easier to hate an institution, anyway, than a father or a mother. Absurdly enough, the authorities in these institutions actually came to respect, even admire, us for our lack of cooperation. Maybe they thought that was how the new elite was supposed to behave. Maybe they thought that, if they tolerated our nonsense, we would cut them a piece of the action.

This tacit form of praise completely inflated our

egos. We felt like monarchs, founding a new king-
dom on the ruins of the old. Our courts were our
circle of friends, and we took turns wearing the
crown. We didn't need advisors. The sky was the
limit. In a time when everything was falling apart,
we were the only ones who had kept our nerve.
We had no fear of new things to come.

We hung around on the streets, swore eternal
friendship among empty concrete landscapes, and
staged plays in abandoned factories. We visited our
older friends in their squat houses and built bon-
fires in the courtyards, grilling vacuum-packed
meat from the supermarket on makeshift barbecues.
From the roofs of the houses we gazed down at the
city. We knew that our lives would never again be
so free and easy.

When one of us overdosed, his death made us
feel, more than ever, that we were the chosen few.
Our whole lives were given over to the pursuit of
this feeling. We were organized like a gang, and
combed the shops of the inner cities shoplifting
jeans, bicycles, books, and CDs. One of us would go
into the dressing room, put on three pairs of pants
and march back out, while the rest stood watch and
scouted for the quickest exit. We smuggled books
and videos underneath our sweaters. We slipped

CDs from their cases to avoid setting off alarms when we walked off with them.

For us, those years were paradise. We never noticed that we were simply acting out a role that had been played many times before—that of the teenage rebel without a cause. At school, we behaved like self-obsessed artists, tortured by their times; at home we were promising, ambitious students, who never attracted attention or caused problems. Our parents had their hands full enough. Among ourselves, we were kings.


When the United States attacked Iraq in 1991, we marched through the streets a couple of times, holding candles and listening to activists sing *Give Peace a Chance*, but our hearts weren't in it. It was always the same people who slept out on the streets, ostensibly in hope of stopping the war or bringing it to a quicker, more humane conclusion. To us, they were just losers who couldn't find jobs or had nothing better to do than sit around in student committees and debate.

Political activism had become suspect. We preferred to spend our time earning money. We no longer saw any need to develop strategies for negotiating what we did in public and what we thought in private. We had learned that when all people get to speak their minds, no one is left to listen.

A few years later, we were able to view the televised pictures of Milosevic's concentration camps without commentary. We had long since given up the good fight. Some of us still occasionally tossed old clothes in the Salvation Army container outside the supermarket or jotted down the bank account numbers of this or that charity when appeals for donations went out on the nightly news, but we no longer felt responsible for all the tragedy and injustice in the world. Our world had gotten a lot smaller, and that was a relief. We didn't have to join a party and participate in a mass movement to be accepted into university, and we could now sleep in on May 1 instead of celebrating International Workers' Day. Nicaragua, Cuba, and Angola were just three foreign countries among many. When Nelson Mandela was elected president of South Africa, or when someone played a recording of our favorite Cuban band, The Buena Vista Social Club, we felt glad, as you do when you bump into an old school friend you haven't seen in years. But that was as far as it went.

## After the Wall

We had enough on our plates in the '90s without wasting our time with political activism and anti-war demonstrations. The long process of assimilation had begun, and we had become more cautious. By the mid-1990s, we had scaled back our criticism and stopped provoking people. We carefully scrutinized both West German society and ourselves, trying to find ways of making an impression without sticking out like sore thumbs. Our dream was that we would someday hold up our passports with our birthplaces, and others would marvel at how people from Cottbus, Sonneberg, or Wismar could have overcome their inborn disadvantages to achieve such great things.

There was a lot of work to be done before that day. What we lacked, above all, was knowledge. It soon became clear how little we actually understood about the society in which we now lived. One of the biggest problems, ironically, was class consciousness. In West Germany, people sometimes went to extreme lengths to avoid appearing either too privileged or too proletarian. And different codes of behavior seemed to apply to girls and to guys. It was hard to figure out.

It took a long time, for example, for me to understand why a brief flash of anxiety crossed the faces of West German guys when I asked them what their parents did. The question was a loaded one, and my friends would always pause, take a deep breath, put on a somewhat desperate smile and shoot back: Why do you want to know? When I pressed the issue, I got vague responses open to a variety of interpretations. Or they tried to brush me off with responses like, "I'm my father's son, and he wasn't just anybody." No one wanted to give me a straight answer. "I come from a humble background and have had to make my own way in the world" was another favorite response. That always made me think of the "antisocials" in our recycling centers and their children, whom we had tutored at school. But the self-made guys from the West didn't look anything like the children of "antisocials."

With girls it was different. The ones who had taken advanced French in high school—whose handbags were always an affluent chaos of lipstick, pills, driver's licenses, perfume bottles, packs of cigarettes, and condoms—would typically come out with phrases like "And just imagine me, with my background," to distance themselves from any hint of the commonplace. That both impressed me and left me at a loss to continue the conversation. What was that supposed to mean? What kind of a background did they have?

Equally impressive were young women who refused to sit on the floor when the university seminar rooms were overcrowded and who pulled a face at vacation plans that included the words "sleeping bag." Their boyfriends, whom they intended to marry at the age of twenty-six, were all "very aristocratic" with their horses and VW Golfs. In an attempt at some jovial, post-Wall banter, those boyfriends would sometimes ask me what it had been like for me growing up with the proletariat. That always made me picture their fathers as those Western visitors to the Leipzig Book Fair—the ones that we weren't supposed to ask for candy.

I couldn't understand why Westerners, with their thousand hints and intimations, made such a big deal about their backgrounds. The issue had been far simpler in the East. The GDR had been a proletarian state. It never would have occurred to us that our parents' occupations could have been culturally important. In the GDR, everyone's house had been full of whatever books and records happened to be available in stores, and if there was a rock concert we'd all tried to get tickets, regardless of whether we knew of the band. Our entire class had visited the theater three times a year and had gone to the museum even more often. And when the teacher asked who among us regularly borrowed books from the local library, we all had raised our hands

There had been few exceptions to this ideal of a classless state. Our neighbor had an RV and always spent his holidays in style in Hungary or on the Baltic coast. For my parents, those were sure signs that he was either a black marketer, a Secret Police informant, or someone with an over-abundance of Western relatives. But we didn't feel jealous, exactly. We were happy as long as we got to go to summer camp. Summer camp was exciting—even if you didn't like the planned excursions, or the end-less flag-saluting cere-monies, or sleeping twenty to a room, or

A ticket to a concert for young people. The fine print on the back prohibits smoking, drinking, and photography.

drinking chamomile tea every day for two weeks. The only true cause of material jealousy were the care packages from the West. We couldn't help but envy classmates who came to school sporting brightly colored T-shirts, Levi's, and Adidas sneakers with Velcro instead of shoelaces.

In our hearts, we've remained the children of a classless society. Our lives in the Federal Republic are guided by the same beliefs we were raised with in the GDR. If you work hard enough you can achieve anything you want, and everyone succeeds in the end with the right amount of talent and drive. But when I articulate these beliefs to my West German friends, they just laugh, call me naive, and start scouring their circle of acquaintances for evidence that success is a matter of who you were born and not who you've become.

In fact, the West Germans envy us the naïveté that allows us to overlook obvious class differences. It's a mystery to us why they keep asking if they're dressed alright when they're getting ready for a date with someone from an "aristocratic" background. I rack my brains for examples of aristocracy in the GDR. These would be people with the coveted "von" in their last names. TV presenter Karl Eduard von Schnitzler, one of the most adamant defenders of East German Communism after the fall of the Wall, and world champion swimmer Franziska van Almsick come to mind—but neither of them would have made a big deal about how someone was dressed.

In the early '90s, we were pretty open about how our parents earned their money but, as the decade wore on, we became less truthful. The reason was not because our parents—almost without exception—had been forced to change jobs or collect unemployment. We were just fitting in with West German attitudes. Henceforth, we either were middle-class or came from humble circumstances. Our parents suddenly worked in chemicals, construction, or the retail sector. Such phrases didn't really mean anything—we didn't really understand what it meant to say your father used to be a factory director, a judge, or a teacher and is now a jobseeker, an early pensioner, or a trainee. Which was more important? Their status in the old, obsolete system or the new one? And were those who had successfully made the transition really any more enlightened and bourgeois?

Besides, many of our parents had worked in professions that no longer existed or had helped build things that were no longer produced in Europe.

## After the Wall

Whether our parents had been teachers, photographers, rail workers, factory directors, or bakers had no real bearing on our current lives. The main thing was to keep on doing what people wanted us to do or, better still, to keep on doing what we *thought* people wanted us to do.


Few of our former convictions have survived. We no longer believe in the fantasy of a greater sense of community in the East, for instance; something that we were always being told and that we ultimately also ended up telling ourselves.

Before the Wall fell, friends frequently would pop by unannounced. This was not because the GDR was more communal—it was because there were hardly any telephones in private homes, so you couldn't call beforehand to ask about stopping by. The open-door policy was the cornerstone of the later myth that the GDR was a more warm-hearted and supportive society than West Germany. But we actually hated being barged in on—it was an invasion of our privacy. Nowadays, of course, we always call ahead.

Likewise, nowadays we're no more and no less environmentally conscious than anyone else. We keep separate containers in our kitchen for various types of trash, turn down the heat when we open the windows in winter, and don't leave the water running while we brush our teeth. At the same time, we buy mineral water in disposable plastic bottles, chuck out glass ones when we can't be bothered to go to the recycling center, and always change the channel when we see pictures of hippies protesting against nuclear power on television. We ignore no-nukes and animal-rights fanatics who solicit our signatures for petitions on the street, putting on an irritated expression and grumbling that we're in a hurry. Once in a while, we buy a newspaper from a homeless person in the subway, and we usually give Russian buskers a bit of spare change, for old times' sake, but we don't take our hands out of our pockets every time there's an opportunity to do good.

We like keeping our hands where they are. Most things are none of our business. The key questions in our new lives are: Who am I? What do I want? Who can be useful to me? Whom do I need? It's nice not to have all those people around telling us how much society values us and what our responsibilities are. We don't pitch in anymore. We spend our time taking care of ourselves.

## After the Wall

There was one thing we never paused to consider,
either before or immediately after the Wall: What
came before the GDR. In the history lessons we got
as children, everyone was part of the anti-fascist resistance movement. Grandparents, parents, neighbors, everyone. It was a festive occasion when
military veterans came to visit our school, bringing
with them the best wishes of working-class veterans around the world, and lending a bit of world-
historical glamour to our everyday classroom
routine. The Young Pioneers' newspapers were full
of stories of our forefathers' heroic deeds during
World War II. When I imagined the war as a child, I
could only ever picture the people I knew meeting
secretly in courtyards to support the White Rose
and other underground resistance organizations.
Otherwise the war was irrelevant. My world began
in 1945. Before that, or so it seemed, nothing much
had happened.

That view changed a few years ago, while I was at
university, when I met my friend Moritz. Moritz
was a buddy of Jan's, and one summer we all drove
out to spend some time at Jan's grandparents' summer house on the German-Belgian border. "Summer
house" struck me as a strange, bourgeois phrase,
but in Jan's mouth, it seemed so normal, like some-

22. 4. 19. 7 7.

Am 22. April feiern wir Lenins 107. Geburts tag. Er kämpfte für ein besseres Leben der russischen Arbeiter und Bauern.

Am 25. Mai 1919 auf dem Roten Platz in Moskau. Lenin begrüßt die Werktätigen, die angetreten sind, die Revolution zu verteidigen

Another page from our past: "On April 22, we celebrate Lenin's 107th birthday. He fought for a better life for Russia's workers and peasants."

thing he'd learned as baby, that I didn't think very
much about it. As we drove on past Cologne, our
discussion centered around Jan—who described
himself as coming from modest circumstances—re-
membering how his grandmother had loved sitting
in her summer house listening to radio plays and
reading popular novels. I sat in the back seat and let
the others talk. Here, too, modest circumstances
seemed to be a fairly elastic category.

As it turned out, the summer house was a summer apartment, but the mood was high, and no one
seemed disappointed. On the contrary, we were
amazed at how much room the place had. The best
spot was the long, oak table in the living room,
where the windows looked out on the backyard. We
all gravitated there, eating, drinking, talking about
everything under the sun, reading stories out loud
to one another, and playing board games. We rarely
left that table. Moritz always sat next to me. Occasionally I'd steal a glance at him from the corner of
my eye, and when I did, my gaze would fall upon a
family picture that hung above the sideboard. I'd
never seen a picture like that. There was Jan's
grandfather, decked out in a uniform I only knew
from museums and sporting a Hitler mustache. The
picture gave me the creeps and, every so often, I'd

sneak over and turn it to face the wall. But Jan always turned it back round again.

Moritz liked being the center of attention—a quality that I admired—and one evening he began to speak of his family's past. It was already dark; Jan's brother had lit the candles in the windows, and the remnants of the cheese we'd had for dessert were lying on the table. The empty wine bottles had begun to pile up, and I can no longer remember what we were talking about, when Moritz began. But once he had gotten our attention, no one interrupted and my eyes remained fixed on his face. He told of how he had learned that his grandfather had been a member of the Nazi party, and not just any member, but a high-ranking functionary. He said that everyone else in the family knew about Grandpa's past, but that it was something that never was talked about. He said that he never had asked any questions, neither of his grandfather nor of his father, and that he'd decided that it was just one more bit of family history.

After a few moments of silence, in which everyone puffed on their cigarettes, those at the other end of the table began to relate similar episodes from their families. Or from other people's families they knew. I was the only one who didn't have any-

# After the Wall

An exemplary school essay, which begins:
"In this poem, Erich Weinert condemns fascist
provocations in the strongest terms."

thing to say. Nothing at all. I thought about my friends in Leipzig, and it occurred to me that we'd never even broached the topic. We didn't know, of course, whether our grandparents had opposed or supported the Nazis. We had been born as children of the present into a country that now belonged to the past, and that had relieved us of such unpleasant questions and answers. I looked around the table and tried to memorize the others' faces. Their hair, their eyes, their noses—everything about them. For the first time, I felt that German history was my history. My friends all knew that they were the grandchildren of the Third Reich. Now I knew it, too. I was one of them.

# 6. The World Is Our Oyster:

## On Love and Friendship

Among the many things that I've lost is the significance of December 13—the day on which my Young
Pioneers brigade celebrated the anniversary of its
founding. I used to circle the date on my calendar,
and, the night before, I'd be so nervous I couldn't
get to sleep. I'd keep getting up to check whether
my Pioneer blouse and scarf were laid out on the
chair next to my bed. Tomorrow was the big day
and I wanted to look my best.

My brigade would gather in the early hours of
the morning in front of our gymnasium. It was always freezing—our blouses and scarves would be
hidden under thick winter jackets. Finally, the
teachers would call us to order and tell us to march
into the building in a dignified fashion. In changing
rooms that smelt of toilet cleaner, we would remove
our street shoes—which even on this, our day of
days, were forbidden in the gymnasium—and put

on sneakers. Then we were supposed to march in perfect time through the narrow back doors and into the sports hall. Although we'd been through hundreds, maybe thousands, of drills, our ceremonial entrance never came off as flawlessly as it was supposed to. Someone had always forgotten his sneakers at home and had to march in his stocking feet, inevitably slipping and falling on the smooth hardwood floor and dragging at least two other classmates down with him.

The best students would receive Pioneer merit badges, and then we'd all salute the flag and spend a few nervous hours in classes. Afterward, the school would gear up for a magnificent celebration. The teachers and school attendants would hang garlands otherwise reserved for the finals of the school mathematics and Russian competitions. They would push aside the benches in the first two floors of classrooms and put up signs on the classroom doors inviting us to come in and paint, construct something from cardboard, or enjoy a cup of tea from a Soviet samovar. A bench would be placed sideways across the stairs, barring our access to the third floor; this was the gateway to paradise. At four P.M., the bench would be removed and we would be allowed upstairs for the highlight of the day's festivities: the official Pioneer dance in the school's auditorium.

You had to be patient. Even as giggling girls shot through the hallways like bottle rockets and the guys gathered, conspiratorial and cool, in front of the school entrance, you couldn't go to the dance before quarter past four. Not unless you wanted to make a fool of yourself and hang out with the little kids from the second or third grade. I always tried to put the waiting interval to good use. I'd sneak off to the toilets with a bundle under my arm. Protected from the prying eyes of the school attendants, I'd secretly slip another top on under my Pioneer blouse so that later, after the first few dances, I could casually take off the blouse and toss it aside.

I had waited all year for these three hours in the school auditorium. With practiced calm, I'd sit on one of the windowsills, something normally not allowed, and swing my legs as I awaited Sascha, the cutest boy in my class. He wore his hair short in the front and long at the back of the neck. He got mediocre grades and was a soccer star. Here was my plan: Sascha and I would dance together in front of all the girls in my year, publicly displaying the love that we felt for one another but that we had previously kept secret, even from ourselves.

## After the Wall

The plan never quite came off. Sascha never asked
me to dance. Every year he ended up with some
other girl from my class, and I was left to stuff my
Pioneer blouse into my school bag and go home
early. Alone. Nevertheless, I loved Sascha throughout those last, long years of the GDR, and no setback
could discourage me from pursuing my passion.

Then suddenly, Sascha was gone. One day in late
1989 or 1990 he simply failed to turn up at school.
A week passed with no sign of him. All the girls
kept tabs on what he was up to and whom he was
currently seeing, and slowly we came to realize that
our worst fear had come true: Sascha had absconded
to the West with his mother. He'd left us behind. He
wouldn't be coming to Pioneer dances any more.
What was worse, that he had never hinted to me
about his plans, or that our young love had come to
such a quick and tragic end?

To my surprise, I later found out that Sascha felt
exactly the same way I did. Two weeks after his dis-
appearance, I got a letter from him. It was my first
love letter composed with a coveted Western Pelikan fountain pen, and he'd included some Western
stickers as well. He wanted to see me. Could we
meet up in a few weeks on Leipzig's central square.

The story of our date can be told quickly

Cosmonauts in love.

enough. In all the years of my secret love, I had never spoken with Sascha as long as I did that day, and I was disappointed. He looked different. He was dressed from head to toe in Western clothes and he had a trendy new hairstyle. I was surprised to find that he already spoke like a West German. He carried himself differently, too.

After screwing up the nerve to admit that all through the years he had secretly been in love with me and me alone, he asked if he could hold my hand. If I remember correctly, I let him. I was curious about how it would feel to hold hands with a boy. But when he asked me to go out with him, I'd had enough. Who did he think was, asking me that, after all the years I'd waited? And how did he think it was going to work? Did he really think I was going to hop a train to the nearest border crossing every Saturday after school, spend the night in a hotel, and then go back home on Sunday? I was twelve years old! After that, whenever he wrote me a letter, I threw it away, unopened. I swore that I never again would fall for a West German.


Another of the many things that are not the same since the Wall fell is vacation travel. Before, every year, when my parents asked my sisters and me where we wanted to spend our summer holiday, our answer was always the Baltic coast—just as we always hollered for macaroni, tomato sauce, and bologna, when they asked us what we wanted for dinner.

My father would pretend not to have heard, and my mother would always look at us with desperate resignation. She knew it would be her job to pester the notoriously unfriendly union authorities who allocated camping spots—in vain. We never got a spot anywhere near the coast, let alone on the water.

Few East Germans ever made it to the Baltic Sea, although a lot of us did get stuck somewhere halfway between there and home, which is probably why it seemed to me that we were always on our way to the GDR's only major body of water. Every year, our parents would try to console us with the hope that maybe next summer we would finally get to see the coast. We never did.

The Baltic coastline still held a special place in my childhood. Even today, the German state of Mecklenburg is for me what Tuscany is for other people. I wouldn't trade the Baltic beaches for the entire Côte d'Azur. My voice still quivers with

Nude sunbathing was a favorite pastime in the GDR—
even though the standard backdrop of postwar housing
developments left something to be desired.

excitement when I tell my friends I'm planning to
spend New Year's Eve on the Baltic island of Use-
dom or my summer on the beaches of Rügen. My
eyes light up even more than if I were going to visit
New York or Barcelona. Anyone can go to New York
and Barcelona, as long as they have the money but,
for me, the Baltic Sea is a magical destination. The
first time I saw it, I felt like one of the chosen people, and I'd still rather visit the eastern coastline

than anywhere else I've been in the past fifteen
years.

The trips GDR citizens took to West Germany before the fall of the Wall were, in contrast, banal. The
destinations were selected neither for their historical significance nor their natural beauty, but for
their proximity. We went to wherever was nearest,
whether that meant Bad Hersfeld, Hof, Goslar, West
Berlin, or Lübeck. Strange vacations. My family's
trips would begin at an ungodly hour in the morning, and our first stop was always a bank where we
would exchange East German for West German
marks.

Back then, it was a relief to know that most of us
would be allowed only one visit to West Germany
in our lifetimes. There was no time to get to know
the place from the inside and, as a rule, we hardly
said a word to the natives while we were there.

Little did we know that a frenetic age of travel
stood directly before us. In the year between the fall
of the Wall, in November 1989, and Germany's official reunification in October 1990, people began to
set up exchange programs. In the spirit of openness,
the West was now our friend. We traveled to our

new partner cities as members of the choir, the Christian youth organization, sports teams, and debating clubs. These were true voyages of discovery. For the first time, we slept in West German beds and took showers with West German water. If you were lucky, your host parents would pick you up and drive you around in their Mercedes, and then, over dinner, explain the difference between peas and carrots. Of course we had peas and carrots in the East. Our West German hosts simply had no way of knowing what we did and didn't know about their country, so often they assumed that we knew nothing at all. On the other hand, they didn't know anything about East Germany. As far as some of them were concerned, we East Germans had survived on bread and water alone, lived in tents, and rode around on donkeys.

After reunification, we no longer went on exchange programs to partner cities such as Hanover or Schweinfurt. Our teachers had connected as much as possible with their West German colleagues and, truth be told, they had probably grown a bit sick of all the meetings to encourage mutual understanding. So instead we ventured further afield. We took class trips to other countries in Western Europe. With money suddenly available from the European Union, I got to go with my Latin class to Italy, with my French class to Paris, and with my English class to London. Because there was invariably cash left over after the trips, those who had participated were always given dictionaries as presents.

The trips were how I got to know the Tower of London, the Forum Romanum, and the Champs-Élysées and began to consider myself a citizen of Europe before most of my fellow East Germans did. The first of my friends were already traveling on Interrail tickets to Portugal and Ireland. More adventurous souls sent postcards from Goa parties in India or kibbutzes in Israel—and threw huge goodbye parties before going off to college in the United States.

I was amazed at how we suddenly took it for granted that the world was our oyster. Sometimes, when sitting down to dinner with French kids as part of some exchange event, I would remember how, in the old days, children of Western European Communists would sometimes be invited to spend their summers at our communal vacation camps. They were always given better quarters than we were, and we weren't allowed to speak to them. I used to watch them from afar, as though they were

# After the Wall

A bill of clean health was required before you were allowed to go to summer camp.

aliens who had suddenly landed on our planet. And I would leave behind love letters, which I knew would never reach their intended recipients, at the ping pong tables. At night I'd lie in my bed at the camp and try to imagine what Paris was like. I dreamed of their brightly colored French sneakers and jogging suits. Then, around midnight, I would force myself to think about the Eastern European kids.

Years later, after the end of the Cold War, some Dutch acquaintances of mine, who had also spent a summer at an East German vacation camp, couldn't believe their ears when I told them how we used to eavesdrop on their conversations. We had longed for nothing more than someday to fall in love with someone who dressed as stylishly as they did. That always made me sad. I knew that, for me, as a citizen of the GDR, a trendy Dutchman was out of the question.

The artificial distance between us and these Western European representatives of fashion was removed in 1990. Nonetheless, it took a couple of years for the Cold War in my head to end so that I could even entertain the idea of one of them and one of us falling in love. Initially, I was freaked out by the idea that some hunky guy from a Western advertisement could now be pursuing a degree in Communication Studies at the Humboldt University in East Berlin. My Socialist education was difficult to shake. Could it really be true that nice people had grown up in a system of capitalist exploitation, empty materialism, and indifference toward world peace and starvation in Africa? People with whom, if everything went well, even I could fall in love? I knew about the libidinous reunification parties older friends of mine had thrown in squat houses, aimed at getting the guests intimately acquainted with people from the other side. The parties were the stuff of legend, with people traveling from as far away as southwestern Germany to get in on the action. But I still didn't believe that kids raised in the material comfort of the West could feel the same intense emotions that we did. If they acted that way, they had to be posers.

I could never fall in love with one of them—no matter how many stories the magazines at the supermarket checkout published about the first mixed marriages. When I started university, West Germans simply got on my nerves—or maybe I just wanted them to get on my nerves. They insisted on giving a stupid answer to every stupid question in seminars, and every time one of us opened his or her mouth and didn't speak in dialect, our thoroughly cowed East German professors would think we came from "over there." At lunch, West Germans would stand in front of the cafeteria to try to get us involved in this or that committee, trying to enlighten and politicize us, to shake us from our typical East German lethargy. I would always walk faster and look off to the side with exaggerated disinterest whenever someone tried to hand me some cheap, photocopied flyer.

I'd eavesdrop on them in the cafeteria or in the coffee shop, as they offered one another smug words of mutual encouragement. West German students were always going on about how psychologists had advised them to concentrate on what *they* wanted, to pursue their goals more aggressively, and, above all, to waste less energy worrying about the wants and needs of everybody else. Glancing over at West Germans at the next table, I would wish that, for their sakes, they could somehow see how empty their young lives had been. What had they ever done other than go to school? It was only much later—several years and thousands of photocopied flyers after the Wall—that I began to appreciate the finer points of their boring, postmodern lives. I began to enjoy hearing stories from their world, a world in which there was no enemy, in which people couldn't distinguish between good and evil, and in which the only dates of historical importance were their own birthdays and Boris Becker's first victory at Wimbledon.

Today, you can fall in love with whomever you choose. We can no longer remember how it was back then when things were different. Our parents are the only ones who still think it's strange when one of "us" ends up with one of "them." I no longer

stop to consider whether a potential boyfriend grew
up on the right side of the Iron Curtain, and my former classmates think nothing of kissing a girl from
West Berlin. In fact, it's fun to engage in a bit of pillow talk with your West German lover about your
time in the Young Pioneers, to confess that you
served as the agitator or the treasurer in your GDR
school. West German lovers always smile at the image of us lining up in rows to salute the flag or running around the woods re-enacting the battles of
Communist partisans. They admire us for our former political commitment—at least that's the way it
seems to us.

That's all fine; but when I fall in love, I want to
be able to pretend that my lover was in my class in
school and that the only reason we never met was
because we didn't have the same subjects at the
same time. I wish that our flag-saluting ceremonies
were the same thing as their church services, and
that they were carefully folding up the aluminum
foil from their lunchtime sandwiches for reuse
while I was taking old newspapers to the recycling
center. If my classmates went on Pioneer retreats to
the Black Sea, then theirs worked as au pairs in Bordeaux—what difference did it make? I suppose we
all went through variations of the same things—

while I envied my peers with West German relatives, they envied their fancy classmates who lived
in villas with big back yards, had summer houses,
and rode around with their moms in VW Golfs (the
family's second car). But lying side-by-side, we
wish we had more than that in common. We wish
we were the same. Fifteen years after the Wall, we
don't want to keep chewing over the differences between East and West. There's no point in fighting
over the Communist Manifesto anymore—it would
only risk ruining a good relationship.

There's a woman in my building named Silvia, and
sometimes when we bump into one another in the
foyer or on the stairs, she invites me to her place for
a glass of wine. Silvia is ten years older than I and
comes from the East German city of Halle. I like her
a lot. I've got nothing against her walls, painted
burgundy red and gone over with a toothbrush for
pseudo-rustic texture. Nor have I any objections to
the natural-fiber carpeting on her floors, the spice
rack over her kitchen table, or the build-your-
Spanish-vocabulary calendar in her bathroom. I also
like her boyfriend, a West German named Hartmut,
who works for a state environmental agency and

always wears the same faded gray jacket with black Levi's. Hartmut's specialty is migratory birds, and he can tell fascinating stories about his research.

Unfortunately, though, the subject of Hartmut's research often leads, via various detours, to a heated debate about the ideals of communism, the advantages of a state-guided market economy, and the effects of globalization on the East European workforce. Smoking one hand-rolled cigarette after another, the two of them will argue, trading accusations and prejudices like blows. I'll turn my attention to the spice rack, examining the more exotic herbs and wishing that I'd gone down to get my mail a few minutes later that day so I wouldn't have run into Silvia. Debates like these, as I know from experience, never end up going anywhere.

The list of accusations is long, and the arguments that go with them are nothing new. Hartmut will let his East German girlfriend express her opinions for awhile, before suddenly blurting out that the East German economy was the one that was a hopeless failure, with no chance of being reformed or rescued. He'd be very interested, he'll say, in hearing what Silvia would have proposed instead of the quick economic and monetary unification that took place in 1990. After all, he'll add, it was the East

Germans who had been the big flag-wavers, applauding then Chancellor Helmut Kohl with a fervor that made every self-respecting West German want to lose his lunch. At this point, Silvia will interrupt him, wishing that he would pay attention to what she was actually saying instead of always rushing to judgment. Her wine glass long drained, she'll continue by complaining that it would be better if West Germans would stop seeing themselves as the center of the universe and the measure of all things. Instead of confronting one another, East and West should try to work together to achieve a mutual understanding. And by the way, Silvia would add, every case of East German collaboration with the Secret Police had to be judged individually according to the specific situation.

I keep out of these debates. I skim through the pages of an environmental journal and note the recent publication of an atlas concerning the habitats of various European butterflies. Some 200 species, or 41 percent of the total population, occur only within a single percent of European territory, whereas some 20 species, or 4.1 percent, can be found throughout a third of the continent. Fascinating stuff.

The debate proceeds without any contribution on

my part. We, the younger generation, don't debate politics with our West German peers. We've agreed to disagree. We don't deny that conflicts exist between East and West, but we're not interested in discussing them. Our memories of the GDR are fading anyway; it's too long ago, and we were too young to remember. We know that our stories about the country where we were born are now shot through with stuff we've since read or seen on TV—what's the point in arguing about them?

These days, the only time I do feel like getting in an argument is when guys who consider themselves politically informed, who read newspapers and wear suits—guys who could be potential boyfriends—lean over in some trendy bar and murmur explanations for their perceived disinterest in what they always call the "former GDR." They're not at all indifferent, they say. They know plenty of people who were born in the five new federal states, and it's not as if they haven't had lots of late-night discussions in which they exchanged their contradictory opinions and experiences with their East German friends. It's amazing, the things they've learned. But they've come to the conclusion in the meantime that there's nothing left to say, that all the old resentments have been dealt with, and that everyone now finds the topic a bit boring.

Such attitudes always makes me think of the West German author Martin Walser and his controversial thesis, presented just before the millennium, that it was time for Germans, fifty years after the Holocaust, to put the past behind them. I take a deep breath, sip on my drink, and get ready to leave the bar. It's been fifteen years since the fall of the Wall, and I've just about run out of ammunition. I have no desire to tell young men in suits for the umpteenth time that they should stop telling us that East German history is finished and just let us decide when, and if, we want to put our past behind us. We may stride proudly through the new glass dome of the reunited Reichstag, but we also identify with the Monument to the Soviet Soldier in Treptow Park, where some 5,000 Russian troops are buried. But, by the time I think of mentioning this, I've already left the place, and the young men in suits have turned their attentions to someone else.

# 7. The Most Important Thing Is to Win:

## On Phys Ed and Sports

The undisputed pinnacle of East German sports achievement was the GDR's 1–0 victory over West Germany in the preliminary round of the 1974 Soccer World Cup. Of course, none of us witnessed Jürgen Sparwasser's famous goal; we were too young, many of us weren't even born yet. And so it was always a little hard to believe our parents when they told us that the GDR used to take part in the World Cup, and that we were the ones who had beaten the mightiest team on the planet. When we were growing up in the '80s, the GDR team wasn't good enough to qualify for the tournament. Every time that my phys ed teacher would go on about the fantastic atmosphere in that miraculous 74th minute in Hamburg Stadium in 1974—one he had only experienced in front of the TV—he would add sheepishly, just before the bell rang, that, of course, West Germany had gone on to win the tournament. We

children breathed a sigh of relief. The winners remained the winners. Nothing had happened to dis-
rupt the usual course of history and our picture of
the world.

Not so with other sports. Ironically, our childhood was the period of the GDR's greatest Olympic
victories, and yet we seldom had the opportunity to
cheer our athletes on. The 1980 Moscow Olympics,
which the United States boycotted, were a total
blowout, but we were too young to really remember
them. So, we were terribly excited in the run-up to
the 1984 Games in Los Angeles. Finally, we were old
enough to follow the medal standings on our own,
and because we'd already won more medals than the
United States in the previous summer's track and
field world championships, we were sure that 1984
was going to be our year. Then came the retaliatory
boycott. We were devastated. Even though it had
been explained to us that the United States was an
evil place and that it was probably better for our
athletes to stay home—given the high rates of crim-
inality in the areas around Los Angeles's Olympic
Village—I was still desperately unhappy. Wrapped
in a blanket on our sofa at four A.M., I watched one
Western athlete after another mount the winners'
podium to receive their medals. By the end of the

The 1972 Munich Olympics were such a big deal in the GDR that our parents took pictures of their TV sets.

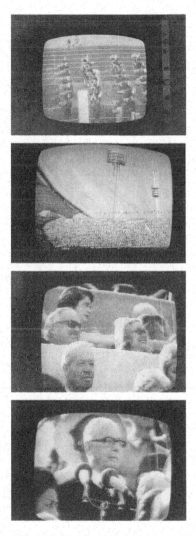

competition, I knew our enemies' national anthems better than I did our own.

By the time the Seoul and Calgary Games came around, our lives had taken a different direction. We straddled the fence; we could acknowledge, in the safety of our own homes, that the West wasn't really the enemy—that was just official propaganda. It was no longer weird to root for West Germans when they were better than our own athletes. The main thing was that a German won. One minute we'd be pulling for East German ski jumper Jens Weiss-flog, swimmer Kristin Otto, or figure skater Katarina Witt;

the next we'd be cheering on West German tennis stars Boris Becker and Steffi Graf—whoever best represented Germany in a given sport

By 1990, with everybody feverishly awaiting reunification, we'd long since started wearing Western sneakers and sportswear. But when West Germany won the World Cup that year and coach Franz Beckenbauer announced that, thanks to its new East German reinforcements, Germany would be basically unbeatable in the future, we began to regard always winning as somewhat suspect. Disgusted by what seemed to us to be the jingoistic behavior of the fans, we turned the TV off before the West German national anthem was played. What we didn't know then was that the fall of the Wall a few months before marked the end of our decade of triumph. It was a period that we would remember for the rest of our lives—ten years on the winning side.

The GDR did everything it could to ensure sporting excellence. The state spent millions on coaches—"sports functionaries," as our parents contemptuously called them—who had nothing else to do than to measure our young legs, muscle mass, speed, and durability. As soon as we could walk, we were assigned to a sport in which we were expected one day to excel, maybe even to bring home gold medals for the greater glory of the nation.

There is hardly one of us today who doesn't have a stack of certificates or a pile of medals lying around somewhere in a desk drawer or a box in our parents' attic. The medals, attached to light-blue strips of cloth printed with the three letters of our country's name, weighed as little as our national currency and were probably equally worthless. But I didn't know that back then. To me, those medals were priceless. I hung them from my bedpost. They made me feel that we were among the victors, part of a seemingly infinite community of triumphant heroes.

My first encounter with a sports functionary came one day when an athletically built stranger suddenly appeared in our grade school. What impressed me most was the fact that he got to wear his Adidas sneakers wherever he liked. (We were only allowed to wear sneakers in the gym.) For hours the man sat on a bench during our gym class, silently taking notes. Every once in awhile he would disappear with one student into the teachers' lounge— a place we only ever saw if it was our turn to write up protocols for the class scrapbook or to get magnesium powder for the parallel bars. My private encounter went like this: The man sat down behind a desk, told me to take a seat, and started asking questions. He wanted to know where my parents worked, if I liked sports, and if I was interesting in visiting his training camp. My friends Manuela and Adriana already attended, and we could train there together during school vacations. The camp was a lot of fun. There was great team spirit. In my case, he said, he thought he could get a lot more out of me. The happy fact was that the state spared no expense to achieve athletic excellence, as it should. Surely I agreed, said the man.

Nothing ever came of this contact. I was flattered when the man led me away to the teachers' lounge in front of my classmates—it was a honor to be allowed in such close proximity to someone with those three Adidas stripes on his sneakers. But my parents had told me not to agree to anything—especially not to join the man at his training camp. And to insure I did as they said, they had signed me up without my knowledge for a tennis club. The athletic functionary scoffed when he heard this, saying tennis was a bourgeois sport with no future. If I thought I would be allowed to travel abroad to play in tournaments, I could get that out of my head im-

One of our national athletes in the latest East German sports attire.

mediately. I should reconsider his offer. But there was nothing to reconsider. It was the beginning of the end of my sports career.

No one explained to me the rationale of tennis as an excuse to avoid state-sponsored sports, and I was green with envy when I saw my classmates going to practice every afternoon, all dolled up in the latest athletic gear. They were always walking around with these huge equipment bags slung over their shoulders and talking about their teams. I wanted to be one of them. I tried to figure out the magic formula by which the sports functionaries could tell which of the schoolgirls would turn out bigger and stronger than the rest, with man-sized shoulders and physiques. I never did figure it out. My one consolation was that these girls always seemed to break out in acne just like our female athletes on TV. I could live without that. Real winners don't have zits.

## After the Wall

Tennis was not one of the privileged disciplines
in which the state took an active interest, but
throughout my childhood I was stuck with it, and it
with me. There were no indoor tennis courts in the
GDR, and so in the winter—at eight o'clock every
Sunday morning, when no one else was using the
place—we practiced our ground strokes and serves
in a hardwood-floored gymnasium. We had to bor-
row a volleyball net because we didn't have one of
our own, and the place was so decrepit that plaster
would flake from the walls every time a tennis ball
bounced off one. Facilities like this were good
enough for a sport that had a reputation of being
not only bourgeois but even slightly fascist. Need-
less to say, there were no tennis training camps.
And if you wanted to exchange your old wooden
racket for a graphite one, you had to go through the
black market in Hungary, dropping the equivalent
of a month's wages in the process.

I wasn't a star. I was not going to win any great
victories for the state, or even any lesser ones for
myself—as I was forced to admit in 1990, when
Jana Kandarr wiped the court with me in less than
half an hour at the GDR junior championships in
Cottbus. As we shook hands at the net and I con-
gratulated her, I was already considering what I was

going to do with the rest of my life now that my
athletic days were over.

Jana Kandarr no doubt quickly forgot about me,
and I never thought I'd see her again, although I
kept tabs in the newspapers on where she was playing and how she was doing. Luckily for her, the
Wall came down soon after those junior championships and she moved from Halle to the West German city of Karlsruhe. For the first time in her life,
at the age when Martina Hingis and Jennifer
Capriati were already playing in international tournaments, Jana was able to attend a real training
camp, one where the plaster *didn't* peel from the
walls when struck.

It was her goal to become one of the top fifty
players in the world and, to her credit, Jana did. It
was 2002, twelve years later, and Jana Kandarr and
I were both in Paris. We didn't meet in person, of
course. I only saw her smiling face in the sports
pages of newspapers reporting on the French Open.
But her image instantly made me feel more at home
on the banks of the Seine. For one night, she was
the star of the tournament, and I knew her! As an
unknown German qualifier, she had knocked out

## After the Wall

Amélie Mauresmo, the number-one-seeded hometown favorite, in the first round.

The next day, I appeared at my boss's desk—the same boss who prided himself on buying a sports paper without his secretary's help—and told him the story of how I had played against Kandarr in Cottbus. Of course, I neglected to mention how long the match had lasted and what the final score had been. I don't think my boss ever listened to me as hard as he did that morning. A short time later, when a brief article about the history of tennis in the GDR appeared in one of the papers, I no longer thought about the sports functionary and the plaster coming off the gymnasium walls. Suddenly, I was proud to have been among the East Germans who had turned out every Sunday at eight A.M. to pound fuzzy yellow balls.

Athletes are the only idols from our generation. It now seems to me that becoming an icon for reunited Germany is the highest achievement an athlete can aspire to. Jana Kandarr never achieved this status. The only two athletes who did were champion light heavyweight boxer Henry Maske—who was much older—and swimmer Franziska van Almsick.

## The Most Important Thing Is to Win

Franziska van Almsick remains our great role model. Van Almsick doesn't like being called Franzi, she prefers Franz; and regardless of what the tabloids say, she's remained one of us. At the same time, she's everything we want to become. We forgive her for cruising around New York City in a new car and for endorsing an East German cosmetics company. She's the new face of East Germany. Our new face. She is younger than many and has gone farther than all. She's the first East-West German sports star.

In 1992, while I was still trying to remember that Madrid is the capital of Spain, van Almsick brought home two silver and two bronze medals from the Olympics in Barcelona. One month later, at the European Junior Championships, she won six gold medals—coming out on top in nearly every event. Van Almsick set three world records in Japan in early 1993, and won five German titles that summer. Reunified Germany finally had the heroine it needed. Franz was as important as Chancellor Helmut Kohl, Western subsidies for the East, and the national soccer team put together—she made us proud.

Franz was the girl we'd all been waiting for. Born in 1978 in East Berlin, at the age of seven she became the youngest swimmer ever invited to join the GDR national team. Four years later, and before she knew it, she had become the embodiment of the new nation.

In the run-up to the 1996 Olympics in Atlanta, van Almsick made the sports pages of the New York Times as "Franzi von Germany," but the sense of novelty was wearing off. The mood in Germany was turning sour; polls showed that East Germans felt like second-class citizens. Franz went to the Games, as sports commentators say, expecting to achieve glory, but she returned with a disappointing two silver medals and one bronze. "I'm not a child prodigy," the young millionaire announced to the assembled journalists. Her coach denied that she needed a therapist, saying that his was all the advice she needed. Meanwhile political pundits said that the poll results prove that great expectations always open up the possibility for bitter disappointments. They were talking about East Germans in general, not Franz, but the point was much the same.

Franz gradually slipped from the public eye. In 1996, for the first time in four years, she wasn't named female Swimmer of the Year. She was approaching something close to, for her at least, oblivion. The important thing, as those responsible for our physical education in the GDR always told us, was to participate, have a good time, and win. Franz taught us how to come out on top; and a bit later she taught us how to lose—that, too, we've learned from reunified Germany's first sports idol.

Things really were different when we were kids. Back then, athletes just went to practice; they didn't have to give daily interviews to a hungry media. They went quietly to the Olympics and afterward, if they won, they were invited to have lunch in their geeky track suits with Party bigwigs and to relive their memories of glory on the *Sport Aktuell* TV show. If you were Katarina Witt, then you might get a guest appearance on a variety program, but that was as far as it went. In East Germany, everyone had a job to do, and an athlete's job was to win. That was what they got paid for; and before they

A certificate confirming that I'm a Level-3 swimmer.

started losing, they retired. No one thought they were stars. In retrospect, I can't help thinking that the old system made more sense.

# 8. Go West, Young Man:
## On Our Future

When Conservative Chancellor Helmut Kohl tried to get himself reelected for a fourth term in 1998, he was counting on East Germany's help. After all, his reunified friends had led him to victory four years previously. "World class leadership for Germany" was his slogan, while his Social Democrat chal lenger, Gerhard Schröder, promised "not to change everything, but to change some things for the better." The streets were plastered with campaign posters. It was awful—when I went to the bakery in the morning, I was half afraid that Schröder would jump up from the counter and throw his arm around my shoulders for the perfect photo op. A dozen reporters with television cameras would storm the place, eager to record the happy interaction between a politician and a member of the constituency. Or maybe the automated bottle return machine in the supermarket would go on the blink and Kohl would appear to take over the job by hand.

There was nothing these candidates wouldn't do to get elected. I can still remember a televised debate staged in the East German city of Magdeburg. There were a lot of kids in the audience, trying their best to look interested. As I tuned in, a young boy, maybe twelve years old, wearing a baseball cap was holding an endless lecture about everything that had changed for him and his friends—mostly for the worse. Before the fall of the Wall, he complained, a day pass to the pool only cost seventeen cents. Now, he couldn't afford to go to the movies, and his local youth center had been closed. The boy didn't say that he could remember the days of a Young Pioneers' clubhouse on every corner, but he certainly seemed to be nostalgic for that bygone age. I had to ask myself whether someone that young would recognize a photo of Erich Honecker if he saw one. Helmut Kohl was apparently thinking much the same thing. Mustering all the patience he could, Kohl began to lecture the boy about his new-found freedoms—freedom to travel, freedom of expression, and the new system of free elections in which every citizen could vote for the party of his choice. But when the boy tried to interrupt him,

Kohl had had enough. "Just how old was this kid," the Chancellor hissed to the event moderator, "when the Wall came down?"

The GDR didn't simply disappear. It didn't take its hat and go, as many people thought it would after the Wall fell. The GDR transformed itself from an idea into an environment—a contaminated environment that you only voluntarily set foot in if you stood to earn some money or if you didn't get accepted to university somewhere else.

This environment was where we grew up. We call it the "zone," affectionately appropriating the scornful West German expression for East Germany—West Germans saw the GDR as a pseudostate that was really nothing more than an area of Soviet occupation. We're aware that this zone is little more than the remnant of an idealistic experiment that had failed before we even came into the world. And we realize that we only know the GDR through our parents' anecdotes. But, gradually, we're coming to feel at home with its legacy.

Today's sociologists have chosen to ignore my generation of East Germans (those born in the '70s) as an object of research, preferring to focus on the last "true" kids of the GDR (those born in the late '60s) or on our successors who grew up in the Eastern half of reunified Germany. Social scientists are fascinated by those fourteen-year-old kids' tales of violence, drugs, resurgent racism, and unemployed parents. By contrast, our generation is nebulous and transitional—we're of no use if you're looking for clear evidence for this or that thesis. Our older siblings fit that bill better.

The last "true" GDR kids, according to the social scientists, remain utterly unlike the same age group in the West, however much they may have copied Western lifestyles and behavior. I can still remember older kids back in the GDR listening to The Cure and Depeche Mode, as they styled their hair with beer and sugar water. But their rebellion was only superficial. Their trends amounted to nothing more than a staged performance of individual withdrawal from public life, a refusal to participate, and, to a certain extent, collective boredom. In cliques, everyone looks and feels the same. Internal unity was more important than external individualism. Such was the schizophrenia of everyday life in the GDR. You had to participate without attracting attention, to function within the system without actively collaborating, or supporting, it. All representatives of the state and other public functionaries were viewed with distrust and distaste. So people tended to keep the private sphere—where they could truly say what they thought—strictly separate from the public one. But, to avoid being denounced to the secret police, you also had to watch what you said to whom. You had to really trust your friends.

We younger kids admired how the older ones exaggerated their disinterest in the word "friendship" when they recited the GDR pledge of allegiance at school. It was their muted declaration of independence. but, for the older kids, that was the only public display at their disposal. They didn't want to take on official positions that required absolute loyalty to the system. Instead, they preferred to live unobtrusive, private lives; and in so doing, sociologists say, their development was covert, but nonetheless remarkably conventional.

The 1980s transformed our older siblings into restricted individualists, oriented around the values of family, career, and friends. In other words, they became middle-class bores. We would never spend our free time the way they do—organizing weekend picnics, singing karaoke in bars, and taking ski holidays with ex-classmates from university. For them, the idea of the GDR never went any further than saluting the flag and other required shows of public patriotism—any active display of interest on their part would have been a betrayal of self. Today, they value the private over the public sphere. For them, having a good atmosphere at work is more important than getting a promotion.

Our generation has little in common with theirs, other than a shared place of birth. We're more at ease with West Germans our age—we even fall in love with them. We've also studied abroad. By comparison, East Germans in their late thirties tend to keep to themselves. Sometimes I wonder whether they don't feel a bit lonely, and if that must be why they do everything in large groups. We're different. Although we don't really belong anywhere either, we tend to share tiny bits of our lives with people from all walks of life. We're not afraid of strangers—which has the advantage of broadening your range of targets when you need to bum a cigarette.

When the Wall fell, our older siblings were the same age as we are now. In retrospect, they had already been through a lot of major decisions. They had finished the tenth grade and had to decide whether to go for the university preparation track

in high school. They could begin to work as trainees in a store, a dairy farm, or the state automobile
factory. The guys could go into the military. They
could hitchhike around Poland or Czechoslovakia.
They could buy their clothes in ordinary shops or
in the more fashionable ones aimed at visiting Westerners. They could apply for permission to travel
abroad or even take refuge in the embassies in
Prague and Budapest.

We were not faced with that standard set of GDR
choices. The Wall fell and left our world utterly confused. We were just becoming teenagers when suddenly everything started spinning around us. We
were too young to understand what was happening,
and too old not to understand that big changes were
in the making. Our childhood was taken away from
us before we even realized what childhood was.
Whereas our parents were robbed of their illusions
of certainty, and our older siblings retreated ever
further into their private lives, there was never anything for us to hold on to. Our memories of the GDR
are almost exclusively private ones. We went
through puberty and young adulthood in the geo-
graphic space that succeeded the old East Germany.
We're the children of a zone, in which everything
was started from scratch, in which things were torn

down brick by brick and in which few of the heady goals of the early '90s have yet been attained. Our entire generation arose because our nation disappeared. That's what defines us: absence.

The only type of change we know is departure. For us, there have never been transitions, only breaks with the past. Our childhood seems like yesterday, but yesterday is completely gone. We wouldn't be bothered if the changes amounted merely to a different smell at the bakery or a new coat of paint on the school—but, for us, *everything* has changed. The bakery is gone; the school is gone. It's all been replaced. The only constant in our lives is something we ourselves constructed: the feeling of belonging to a generation.

A generation we will remain. The first decade and a half of freedom has been eventful. We said a lot of goodbyes and made many new friends. Surely the next decades will be calmer, more settled. We are the first West Germans from East Germany, and neither the way we speak, nor the way we behave, nor the way we dress betrays our origins. Our assimilation has been a success—we only wish we could say the same of our parents and the rest of our families.

It frightens us to think that we were but brief guests in our native land. The years before the fall of the Wall already make up slightly less than half our lives, a percentage that will shrink more and more as the years go by. The GDR will recede into the distance, becoming ever smaller and more unreal, like an object in a car's rear-view mirror.

With our hands on the wheel and our butts in the driver's seat, our job now is to leave our childhood behind. We've grown up. We're no longer interested in those bumper stickers that read "The GDR is dead—long live the GDR!" Recently, I found one of Jonathan's old tapes under the passenger's seat of my car. He had given it to me at the beginning of our friendship in Leipzig. With a wink, he said I could learn a lot from it. I didn't play the thing much back then. I could never understand what the Pet Shop Boys were trying to say when they sang "Go West, life is peaceful there." I liked the song about West End boys and East End girls a lot better.

But now, when I'm driving around Berlin, I play that tape over and over. I have to laugh every time these two English guys sing: "We will fly so high. Tell all our friends goodbye. We will start life anew."

## After the Wall

I've thrown away all the junk that was in the
trunk and the back seat. My mother is happy that
I've started keeping the car tidy. The full ashtray
used to bother her so much that she said she didn't
even want to ride with me. Like my friend Jenny, I
enjoy cruising around with the window open, my
arm hanging out and a cigarette butt dangling from
my lips. It makes no difference that the car isn't an
automatic and doesn't have Hamburg plates.

Right now, I'm on my way to Jan's place on the
western side of the Spree River. I'd take the tram,
but the line ends at the bridge that used to be the
border between us and them. East Berlin was always
bigger on trams. It's a mild spring evening, and even
here, in the city, you can smell the trees starting to
blossom. It would be great to sit outside right now
and watch a fireworks display or a soccer match.

I didn't bring my handbag, but I've got everything I need in the pockets of my jeans—my cigarettes, a lighter, a couple of euros, and my car keys.
As I near the bridge that used to mark the end of
one Germany and the beginning of another, I know
that no one will stop me—at least, not to have me
empty the contents of my pockets, but maybe to
bum a cigarette.

# A Note from the Translator

When it was published in 2002, Jana Hensel's *After the Wall*—originally titled *Zonenkinder* in German—became an almost instant best seller. It was a sensation—the first book to explore the trials and tribulations of a generation of East Germans that spent its childhood in the GDR and its adolescence and adulthood in the reunited Federal Republic. Many books about the difficulty of negotiating the East-West divide have followed, but Hensel's stands as the first to define a cultural phenomenon—the alienation and loss felt by the last generation of East German youth after the fall of the Wall. For the American reader, some of the historical and cultural references in *After the Wall* may be confusing, so we offer this brief recap of modern Germany and of the main themes in Hensel's story.

## A Note from the Translator

## A Brief History of East Germany

The GDR was formed in 1949 from the Soviet occupation zone of the former Third Reich. At the same time, the British, American, and French zones in the West joined to form the Federal Republic. East Germany was essentially a one-party state, ruled by the SED or Socialist Unity Party bureaucracy with a despotic state and party leader—Walter Ulbricht (1949–71) and Erich Honecker (1971–1989)—at its head.

Despite its name, the GDR wasn't democratic. Political power was monopolized by the party apparatus, the economy was centralized and state-run in line with Marxist-Leninist ideology, and all major decisions and developments had to meet with the approval of the Politburo in Moscow. Although a great number of its citizens initially embraced the "Socialist experiment," discontent with the government's heavy-handed rule grew quickly. On June 17, 1953, the East German army and Soviet tanks had to be called in to put down a nationwide strike against increases in production quotas and other government policies, making a lie of the GDR propaganda about building a state by and for the working masses.

The GDR owed its existence to the Soviet Union and the Cold War. Although East Germans had the highest standard of living in the Eastern bloc, and while they did develop a sense of national identity, both positive and negative, the GDR was perennially overshadowed by the more affluent capitalist Federal Republic. By the late 1950s, increasing numbers of its citizens "voted with their feet," i.e., absconded to West Germany, where they were treated as a special class of refugees: fellow citizens who had escaped from a repressive illegitimate regime occupying German soil. By 1961, the problem of people fleeing had reached such proportions that it threatened the very existence of the GDR, and the SED took the extraordinary step of sealing off its borders to the West with fortifications and armed guards to prevent its own citizens from escaping. The Berlin Wall became the particularly ugly face of Communist coercion.

With the divide between East and West literally set in concrete, Germans as a whole had no choice but to accept the status quo as a kind of fate. In 1969, the GDR and the Federal Republic formally recognized one another, and East Germans by and large adopted a strategy of "inner emigration," whereby they toed the party line in public in return for being allowed a measure of freedom in their private lives. They may not have liked the system, but they got used to the idea of a paternalistic state bureaucracy that provided for their basic needs and organized their daily lives, as it restricted their ambitions and horizons.

Nonetheless, the potential for rebellion didn't disappear. In 1989, in the wake of reformist Soviet Premier Mikhail Gorbachev's policy of *perestroika* or "openness," a protest movement began to build that saw tens of thousands of antigovernment demonstrators take the streets in cities like Leipzig for what became known as the Monday Rallies. With the Soviets refusing to quash popular discontent by force, the SED was forced to depose Honecker and remove the unpopular restrictions on travel.

The opening of the borders in November 1989— or the Fall of the Wall, as it is often known—spelled the end of the GDR. A year later, after negotiations handled by an interim GDR leadership; the West German government, under Chancellor Helmut Kohl; and the four occupying powers from World War II, East Germans voted to accede to the Federal Republic. The Cold War was over; the GDR, at the age of forty-one, was laid to rest.

What remained of East Germany was a collective identity and culture. Kohl campaigned intensively for "reunification" in 1990, with the visions that the GDR would "blossom with prosperity" if its citizens voted to join and submit to the West German system. The majority of East Germans believed those promises. What they failed to realize was that the mentality acquired under more than four decades of Socialism would often leave them ill-equipped to deal with the everyday demands of a free-market, competitive society. Meanwhile the Federal Republic's boom years were over, and attempts to impose Western German practices and thinking—for instance, by closing factories deemed unproductive—have just as often done more harm than good.

Fifteen years after reunification, Germany is still a country of two halves. Unemployment in the former GDR remains at more than twenty percent, twice as high as in the rest of Germany. Many young people leave to seek their fortunes elsewhere, while the middle-aged jobless—who are too old to be retrained—sink into catatonic resignation, asking themselves what went wrong. The GDR is history. East Germany—as a geographical area, a way of life, and a mentality—survives to this day.

## Jana Hensel and Her Generation

There have been countless books exploring the trials and tribulations of former GDR citizens, who were forced as adults to adapt to life in the Federal Republic. Much has also written about the so-called children of reunification, *i.e.,* today's post-Cold-War German kids. *After the Wall* is the first major book to tackle the generation in between, those who spent their brief childhoods in the GDR and the rest of their lives in the Federal Republic.

Jana Hensel was born in 1976 in Leipzig, the flash point for the Monday Rallies in 1989, and the city that, more than any other, has come to symbolize East German popular rebellion against the GDR. From 1983–90 Hensel attended grade school—the curriculum was set by the SED. In 1991, she progressed to a university-preparation track in high school, where her graduating class became the first to use textbooks that came from the West. In 1995, she began studying French and German literature at Leipzig University. From 1998–99, Hensel spent a year abroad in Marseilles, transferring to the Humboldt University in Berlin upon her return to Germany. Parallel to her studies, she published an Internet literary magazine and worked as a freelance

editor for a major publisher. In 2002, she spent a
year in Paris and began work on this book. *After the
Wall* became an almost instant best seller when it
was published in 2002. Now, at the age of twenty-
eight, Hensel is a nationally acclaimed author, who
has worked for Germany's most prestigious weekly
news magazine, *Der Spiegel*, and toured abroad
everywhere from China to North America. Hers is,
by any standards, a success story, the tale of an "immigrants' daughter" who assimilated into the main-
stream and made it very big indeed.

The irony—one not lost on Hensel herself—is
that her success is intimately connected to her parents' hardships, even their failures. "West Germans
can always ask for parental advice when they get in
trouble or can't make a decision," Hensel says over a
coffee in a trendy café in an East Berlin district that
has been totally re-made by Western entrepreneurs.
"I can't. My parents' experience isn't relevant. They
know far less about this society than I do."

Her book is full of reminiscences and anecdotes
from daily life that illustrate the distance between
East Germans of her age and their mothers and fathers—everything from the awkwardness of exchanging unwanted gifts on holidays to heated
political arguments when parents collide with

friends from the West. The experiences Hensel describes are common to the second generation after immigration, though the parents she describes never actually moved anywhere. Or as Jana Hensel puts it in conversation

> The problem is that my parents are fluent in the language. If they spoke broken German, everyone would understand what they are: refugees from a country that no longer exists, who don't know how to get on in their adopted homeland. And people would also understand that people like me have to negotiate the same situation as the kids of Italian or Korean immigrants to the United States.

The original German title of this book, *Zonenkinder*, translates literally as "children of the zone." The word is a reference to the origins of the GDR in the Soviet occupation zone, a slang expression traditionally used by West Germans to underscore their contempt for the East, and a term ironically appropriated by East Germans to indicate their affiliation with the ex-Socialist community. Hensel also uses it to describe a particular state of mind among people of her generation, a "twilight zone" of sorts, in which daily life seems arbitrary, provisional, and somewhat unreal. Reunification encouraged East Germans to repress the past. East Germans of her generation have succeeded where their parents often failed, but that has left them feeling ill at ease with what amounts to a black hole in their biographies.

## Searching for the Past

*Zonenkinder* was written, in part, as a response to a West German best seller, Florian Illies's *Generation Golf,* and the Western "pop literature" trend of the late 1990s. With its title taken from a Volkswagen ad campaign, *Generation Golf* read like a transcription of an extended cocktail-party reminiscence in the "Hey, remember *Gilligan's Island*"-vein about the cultural detritus of the author's youth. The message, insofar as there was one, was that today's generation of young adults is defined by unquestioning materialism. The book was a massive hit, appealing not only to its target audience but also to older readers curious about how their sons and daughters viewed the world. The only group that was left out were those from the East.

East Germans, Hensel argues, were no less materialistic than their Western peers, and *Zonenkinder* is full of the cultural detritus from her own Socialist childhood. The difference is that the cult products and TV shows of the GDR carry no cultural value for the majority of people in the society where East Germans now live. With considerable self-irony, Hensel describes her disappointment at a college dormitory party in France where the conversation turns to the Smurfs, when she realizes that East German kids' TV shows don't provide any basis for generational bonding.

The feelings of alienation and loss that arise in such moments make *After the Wall* far more interesting than *Generation Golf*. As Hensel describes them, the cartoon mascots of the Socialist Young Pioneers youth group may appear ham-fisted and provincial to readers raised in the West, but it doesn't require a great leap of imagination for us to realize that they leave a gap when they disappear. The artifacts of the mass culture of our youth may be utterly banal, but they do serve to anchor us in place and time—a lesson that applies equally well to East and West and that may inspire Western readers to reflect on the materialism of their own childhoods in a way that goes beyond the mindless celebration of the familiar.

At the same time, Hensel is also writing against

the nostalgic longing for the GDR, a phenomenon known in German as *Ostalgie*. Although it abounds with comic, often affectionate portrayals of the past, *After the Wall* doesn't whitewash life under a one-party dictatorship. In her descriptions of her parents' frantic efforts to procure the necessary supplies for enjoyable Christmas celebrations, or the visit to her school by a Communist "sports functionary" in search of children he can mold into steroid-infused Olympic gold-medalists, Hensel captures the repressive, sinister side of a society based upon sacrificing the interests of the individual to those of the state. Readers get little sense in these pages that things would be better by turning back the clock to the days when common citizens had to stand in lines at meagrely stocked department stores, and the State Secret Police or *Stasi* enlisted a virtual army of informers to spy on their neighbors for signs of potential rebellion.

Hensel wants to recover, not reinstate, the past. "I've grown afraid," she writes, "that by always looking forward and never glancing back, we no longer have any idea where we stand." What's at stake in her reminiscences about the minutiae of a GDR childhood is more than just the pleasant warmth of nostalgia. It's the sense of a collective history that gets temporarily disrupted when people are uprooted and past and present become disjoined.

## The Politics of Memory

Hensel sets up the book as a journey to the past, but confesses in its initial pages that she isn't sure she will be able to "find my way back." Part of the problem is the omnipresence of the media. Her memories of 1989, as she discovers with dismay, aren't so much recollections of the Monday Rallies themselves as of the television news reports about them. Struck by her obvious difference from her Western peers in Marseilles, Hensel decides to pay a return visit to Leipzig to see the city of her childhood with her own eyes. Her descriptions of what she saw and how she felt re-access a number of genuine recollections obscured by the triumphant media images of the Fall of the Wall.

Memory is a political issue in the new Germany. Many West Germans complain that their Eastern countrymen—a decade and a half after reunification—have yet to get over the "walls in their heads," i.e., put their Socialist past and its attendant mind-set behind them. East Germans, on the other hand, find this presumptuous. In a series of satiric anecdotes, Hensel suggests that West Germans' frustration with East Germans' interest in their past is in fact an extension of old Cold-War hostilities and need for control. "I have no desire," writes Hensel, "to tell young men in suits for the umpteenth time that they should stop telling us that East German history is finished, and just let us decide when and if we want to put our past behind us."

There is, however, another set of memories that Hensel first accesses as a student while visiting the summer house of a college friend from the West. There, she is struck by a family photo on the wall of her friend's grandfather wearing an SS uniform. The founding myth of the GDR was one of heroic Socialist resistance to Nazi barbarity. As a result, East Germans had little sense of sharing any sort of collective guilt for the crimes of the Holocaust. In the book's most bitter irony, Hensel realizes that her new "Federal German" identity entails membership in the community of the "grandchildren of the perpetrators." Memory, it turns out, goes further back than she thought.

Hensel's unexpected confrontation with Germany's Nazi legacy is a somber interlude in a book that otherwise treats a serious topic without taking itself too seriously—something Germans, and East Germans in particular, are often accused of doing. *After the Wall* is not a dry sociological study aiming toward a comprehensive, fact-based portrait of a demographic group. It is a witty, ironic, self-deprecating personal narrative that flows freely between the past and the present and focuses on everyday culture: fashion, sports, eating and drinking, and above all social interaction.

Lacking a clear connection to the society in which they were born but were forced to forget, Hensel concludes that today's East Germans of her generation are united by a search for community as they pursue individual success. Bonding with friends takes the place of ties to the past or the family. "The only constant in our lives," Hensel writes, "is something we ourselves constructed: the feeling of belonging to a generation." Uncomfortable as it may have been at first, the "zone" emerges as not all that bad a place to be.

B
B S

PublicAffairs is a publishing house founded in 1997. It is a tribute to the standards, values, and flair of three persons who have served as mentors to countless reporters, writers, editors, and book people of all kinds, including me.

I.F. STONE, proprietor of *I. F. Stone's Weekly*, combined a commitment to the First Amendment with entrepreneurial zeal and reporting skill and became one of the great independent journalists in American history. At the age of eighty, Izzy published *The Trial of Socrates*, which was a national bestseller. He wrote the book after he taught himself ancient Greek.

BENJAMIN C. BRADLEE was for nearly thirty years the charismatic editorial leader of *The Washington Post*. It was Ben who gave the *Post* the range and courage to pursue such historic issues as Watergate. He supported his reporters with a tenacity that made them fearless and it is no accident that so many became authors of influential, best-selling books.

ROBERT L. BERNSTEIN, the chief executive of Random House for more than a quarter century, guided one of the nation's premier publishing houses. Bob was personally responsible for many books of political dissent and argument that challenged tyranny around the globe. He is also the founder and longtime chair of Human Rights Watch, one of the most respected human rights organizations in the world.

·     ·     ·

For fifty years, the banner of Public Affairs Press was carried by its owner Morris B. Schnapper, who published Gandhi, Nasser, Toynbee, Truman, and about 1,500 other authors. In 1983, Schnapper was described by *The Washington Post* as "a redoubtable gadfly." His legacy will endure in the books to come.

Peter Osnos, *Founder and Editor-at-Large*

CPSIA information can be obtained
at www.ICGtesting.com
Printed in the USA
BVOW08s0206110917
494435BV00005B/5/P